USING
Curse Words

Using Curse Words

Finding Unusual Solutions to Life's "Worst" Problems

Myra Fiacco

Filles Vertes Publishing

Coeur d'Alene, ID

IV

Myra Fiacco/Filles Vertes Publishing
PO Box 20175
Coeur d'Alene, ID 83816
www.fillesvertespublishing.com
www.myrafiacco.com
www.usingcursewords.com

Book Layout © 2018 Filles Vertes Publishing, LLC
Cover Design © 2018 Filles Vertes Publishing, LLC
Photography © 2018 Andrea Jensen Photography

Books may be purchased in quantity and/or special sales by contacting the publisher.

Using Curse Words/ Myra Fiacco. — 1st ed.
ISBN 978-1-946802-30-9
eBook ISBN 978-1-946802-31-6
ePub ISBN 978-1-946802-33-0

DEDICATED

to

Tara - my dearest fucking angel.

Ray - the bravest bitch I know.

Chelsea - badass doesn't even begin to describe you.

NAVIGATE
Find Your Shit

DEAR SISTER,
Welp, I done went and died.

Oil and vinegar, peanut butter and mayonnaise, a paper house in the rain—you and I, sister, just don't mesh, which is funny because we're very much alike. We could've been the same person, had our life experiences been identical from birth. But, as it does, life took us down different paths, and those paths made us different people.

We are both fiery and fiercely proud of our ancestry. We're both expressive and artistic, guided by our creative spirits into the kind of art that keeps us up at night, covered in ink (or paint, or acetone, or keyboard callouses). We're both shy when you don't know us and wild when you do. We defend our friends, love others to a fault, and struggle with self-confidence. Heck, we were both born in December in the 80s.

Despite all of the above, our similarities never allowed for a bond to form.

Growing up, our angsty relationship caused a rift, and we never got close enough to connect. I wasn't forgiving and patient like our older sister, and I wasn't calm and bright like our youngest sister. Generally, a "normal" birth order lands the oldest as the leader and the youngest gets away with everything (seriously—what's that about?). That leaves the middle child as the rebel. Except there were two of us in the middle. We were the weird little spotlight-chasers, and instead of championing our mutual fists in the air, we battled each other for position without mercy.

I know I affected the way you grew up—having a sister fighting with you instead of for you. Where I should've protected you and made sure you had a bully-free childhood, I picked on you like it was my job. Ouch, it hurts my heart to say those words, but they're sadly true. I took any opportunity to turn the slightest bit of tension between us into a warzone. I channeled all that childhood and pre-teen angst of mine into this torturous, big-sister attempt at tough love and catapulted it toward you. I was mean.

It's a dreadful burden to bear, knowing I contributed to someone's misery long ago. Since I'm no longer that young (or that person), I choose to no longer feel guilty for the many ways twelve-year-old me held you back. Instead, here comes adult me, and she can remedy hurts and show up in supporting and loving ways.

And so, because I have a lot to make up for, I'm going to take a chance in the right direction and tell you about how I done gone and fucking *died* this year. I'll explain, but first I need to go grab a box of tissues to get through this.

I promise to leave out the blood and gore (there's no blood or gore), but to paint a proper story, I'll need to backup a few months before I died to set the horrific scene.

Last year was hella hard, traumatic even, on my soul. I'd thrown my family into a seemingly endless pit of financial strain by fastening a set of golden handcuffs between myself and my yet-to-be successful small press publishing company. With the pressure of my financial and business decisions weighing on my shoulders daily, I struggled to keep up with the mounds of work I thought were needed to start creating revenue. Because I was buried in work that never ended and I could never seem to catch up on, I formed a new disdain for myself and struggled to be a leader to my team while fighting against this chronic self-hatred.

I let my insecurities hollow me out into a whisper of the courageous, vivacious pioneer I've always sought to be in life. I became the victim of my mind: ugly-crying daily, mumbling about how much I hated life, or struggling to remember simple things like my kids having a holiday from school.

Yes, on top of the shit storm I created in my business, I carried that storm into my home and made life awful for my kids. I yelled way more than was ever necessary, setting expectations high because I was used to doing that very thing for myself. I even stopped doing basic, fun things with them, like reading books and playing. I'll let that sink in for a moment:

I was trying to run a successful publishing company and I *rarely read to my kids*. (Oh, my heart!) In my despair and busyness, while trying to keep it all together, I fell so, so short of the mother my three young children needed.

My marriage, my safe place, also began to decline; there are only so many times a husband can pick his wife up off the floor without letting it weight him down too. Anger became our go-to response for most stressful situations (which, by now, we've determined was happening on the daily), and our fights became epic and deeply cutting.

I even set all my friendships to the side—who has time to nurture others?

Life had fallen apart, and I had set it up to happen.

I saw no way out. Each morning, I woke up to another day of hating. When my phone would buzz as my alarm went off in the morning, the first thought that ran through my mind was that the alarm was an email alert, and surely the email was someone who was angry with me. Since I've only received a handful of those emails in my *life*, I don't even know where that fear came from except from my own self-hatred. THAT was my first thought in the morning for months.

My insecurities mounted, and I dragged myself through the day, frustrated, stressed, and usually with oatmeal in my hair. Everyone needed me, but I was bitter, resentful, and exhausted. So, I treated every interaction with this question at the forefront of my mind: "What do they want me to do for them this time?"

Help was being offered; I chose instead to squander it and wallow in my suffering.

People were trying to support me; I decided my pity party was more fun.

Friends and family admired me; I was too hung up on not being "good enough."

It sucked. Life was heavy all the time. I waited on the beach of life, hail pelting me in the face, lightening crashing over the water. All the elements of a storm threatening to pull me under. And there I was with my raft, determined to fucking sail.

And then, as a tropical cyclone with a wind speed of 3,486 mph does when heading for a pig factory in June, shit blew up. When my home life, business, and heart hung in the balance, I fled.

Following a fight with my husband—after which I thrust the kids upon him and retreated to the basement for some space—I stopped looking down at where I wanted my feet to take me, and I looked up. I spoke a silent prayer to God, and I believe God spoke back to me for the first time ever. (Being pastor's kids, you'd think growing up in the environment of the church I would've heard an "atta girl!" from the big guy by now, huh? Better late than never. Just kidding, I know the timing was just right.)

And it doesn't matter what was said. What's important was that I looked up and saw the size of the universe for the first time. My focus shifted and there were possibilities among an infinite pool of love and grace and kindness pouring out on me. God's hand was obvious in everything: from the magnificent way our brains work, to the beauty of my surroundings. My eyes were open to the way our world works in patterns. Music sounded different, I saw paintings in my house in a new way, and I rediscovered the smiles on my children's faces. I found compassion and empathy for people again—my family especially.

I was quite literally pulled out of the darkness and into the light.

An old self died; "I" passed away.

The "I" I had known for years fell away and I finally got to be myself again. My wonderful, glorious, funny, weird, *alive* self again.

And I finally got it, what it means to be "born again." Not in a church camp, waving our hands to an acoustic rendition of "Open the Eyes to My Heart, Lord" kind of way, (although I'm not dogging that kind of enthusiasm). But no, I mean that a part of me died.

Amputated, caput, disappeared, "see you in hell baby" *gone* from my life.

The further I marched forward and away from this old life, the more I saw this dead part of me as a sort of "dark wizard dying in the white railway station of a certain chosen boy's mind" way. I'd violently kicked this old me to the train platform of my mind, and in her shriveled state, I felt sorry for that old, horrid part of me. I'd amputated her; I said some words with God and decided to let her go. Though I no longer carried the "old me" around, she came back in phantom pains. Nothing ever leaves without a trace, you know. But traces soon disappear, so I marched forward, honoring who that old me was and thanking her for all she tried to do.

I honored her, though I no longer wanted to *be* her. So, I kept moving.

I've worked hard to break old patterns of thought and walk in this newer version of myself, but to be honest, I still stumble and cry. And I definitely want to yell when milk "mysteriously" spills on the couch. I struggle with what the appropriate amount of dread and insecurity over my business risks should be and am not always quick to give myself grace. And truth be told, I often mourn all the wasted time I spent being a wretched bitch. Even then, I forgive myself and turn old lessons into wisdom.

I no longer hate.

A true, physical death may not have been far off if I'd kept up my old life. I could've ended up having a heart attack or liver complications from drinking so much wine or become too depressed to function. But I was already nearly dead inside, and instead of going through the same hollow motions of a walking corpse, I chose to breathe life into my body again.

This is the death I came out of and into life. This is the death I want for you, though I'll never mean it in an "I want you hurt" way. I want you to ask yourself whether there's a dark growth in your mind that grew without your permission, and I want you to wonder why you're holding onto it—why you're letting it suck the life out of you.

Maybe your life—your freedom from that weight—is on the other side of amputating that old you.

Before you wonder if I'm asking you to physically hurt yourself, I'd never. You are a wonderfully, beautifully made human being who should never have to feel that kind of pain. If your internal pain overwhelms your soul with such force that you need to let it out with self-harm or addiction, please reach out to someone you know who can maturely guide you to the help you need. If you don't have that person, there are list of resources at the end of this book for you.

And before you think this is a ploy to get you to sit with me at church or trade your Nine Inch Nails for Christian radio, let me assure you of this: I won't ask to pray a prayer of salvation over you or anything. I'm not going to give you "Jesus Junk." We all like our little notecards with scripture and positive affirmations, but I won't bombard you with tacky religious products like "Testa-Mints" or anything.

I won't barrage you. But I will fight for you.

When you stay up all night working on your beautiful artistic creations, I don't want you to do it while lost in sadness. I want you singing and dancing until your sweet boys fall asleep at your feet, gripping their teddy bears covered in paint splatters.

I want your tears to be an expression of how beautifully you see the world and not because you feel only its crushing weight smashing down every joyous part of who you are.

When you fall in love again, I want it to be with yourself and not with someone who doesn't know your value. (Though I pray every day for you to find a loving, honorable, patient, and amiable Viking-looking dude.)

I'd love for you to see God and the Universe as more than just the version we learned about in youth group. If you could see how the Divine is *in* you—the creator who created you to CREATE, dammit—you might see yourself in the best light instead of that crushing weight of a mental darkness that grows like a tumor

If the part of you that expects the worst in life wasn't there anymore, you might actually be able to *breathe* again. You could look out into the sky and see the wonders of the stars mapped out above you. Dreams would unfold when you'd least expect it. Life itself would feel like a gift of endless possibilities. You would be full of compassion for yourself, empathy for others, and invigorated with love and beauty.

I know, because it's how I feel. After letting that darkness crush me for too long, I let that part of me go, and set myself free.

And for the first time in my life, I want you to have what I have.

Yup, I took away your My Little Ponies when you were a kid. You loved horses so much more than I ever did and I *never* let you enjoy that. I'm sorry. I didn't want you to copy me when we were teenagers. You probably thought I was the shit (fingers crossed) and just wanted to be like me, and I made you feel like a copycat. I'm sorry, you didn't deserve that. And I resisted hard core when you showed similar interests as me in early adulthood; I thought it meant you were taking my identity. I shouldn't have done that, I should have fought for you and lifted you up. I'm sorry I never wanted you to have what I had.

But THIS. This is *the* part of me that I wish I could give you. If I could, I'd bottle it into medicine and sing a special song convincing you to take it. I can't though. Nothing good ever came from forcing anything down someone's throat. This beautiful perspective can't be thrust onto anyone, though I would live my "year from hell" all over again if it meant you could see what I see.

If you're ready to let go of the spiritual, emotional, or mental tumor that has weighed you down, I'm here to help. I'll stand by your side in the train station and lament as it shrivels, and then we'll walk into the light together. I'm here whenever you're ready.

Although it took us thirty-plus years to "get along," I've always loved you.

And I love you so much that I can't watch you live a life of death before your heart stops beating.

I want you to let that part of you die so you can fully come back to life, come back to us.

I love you always,

INTRODUCTION
Fucking Magic

What's your favorite curse word?

Come on; you have a preferred, go-to string of profanity—the one you save for just the right moment. Have it in your mind? Good, save it there, you'll get to let it out in a minute.

We love using curse words, don't we?

In the right situation, they can roll off our tongues like a crunched-up bite of anger. "Son of a bitch!" we rage into the night when the world falls apart around us. "Mother fucker!" we scream at the table leg when we slam our baby toe into the sharp edge. The struggle is real.

And curse words feel good to say. Expressing our emotions through curse words is like a verbal detox. Of course, we don't want to say them at the wrong times—weddings and funerals are generally frowned upon venues to share these words, as are job interviews and around small children. We don't want to overuse them until they lose their luster. In moderation and used appropriately, curse words can be cleansing and, honestly, a little fun.

But you know what isn't fun? Defining ourselves by curse words:

"Fuckup."

"Lazy Ass."

"Piece of Shit."

Gasp!

I know, we can be mean to ourselves. It's downright awful what our internal negative committee can scream on repeat into our minds. Even if you don't identify with those harsh curse words, you probably have curse words of your own that you don't even realize you define yourself by.

Maybe you call yourself…

"Anxious."

"Exhausted."

"Disappointed."

"Stuck."

We define ourselves with words that won't ever serve us and then wonder why our lives feel broken, unfulfilled, and incomplete.

Instead of looking outside for a quick fix to our broken world—only to have to do it again tomorrow—we can pull these curse words out at the root, solving the problem from the inside. But the solutions we often think will work aren't always valid, they're just popular.

We're told that in order to avoid disappointment, we need to work our asses off to get the result that will make us happy. That isn't the solution at all. We believe that to be less lonely, we must pour into others until we're clean out of energy, so they'll give love back to us, but that doesn't work, does it?

We think we know how to fix what's wrong with our lives, but we don't actually have the right solutions, so we end up battling the same "curse words" on repeat.

I've been devoted to understanding the endless fascinations of the human spirit since I was gazing at the world from my tippie toes. I love understanding what makes us tick, what motivates us, and what helps us grow. In short, I want to live the best life I can, and I'm passionate about positive change for myself and others.

I'm a pusher, a striver. And this has always served me well in one way or another. But nothing could've prepared me for the shock of opening a startup company. Not only did I jump in over my head with a heavily involved business model, I chose one of the fastest declining industries to pursue: I opened a traditional publishing house in a world where publishing has become over-saturated, and readers seem to be on the steady decline in favor of more interactive forms of entertainment.

Regardless of the digital movement, I couldn't shake this monumental dream that I could help readers fall in love with books again, even if our platform wasn't worldwide. I envisioned investing in the production of literary masterpieces to fulfill the dreams of fellow strivers like myself. Unfortunately, the dream came with very little skill, knowledge, or background, and I soon discovered I had started a slow climb up my personal Mount Everest.

I could barely keep up with my family life and let the balance crumble around me. I was letting the failures of my life win, and it was scary. Like, fake-my-death-and-flee-to-Puerto-Rico-and-change-my-name-to-Bianca scary. (Yeah, it was easy to feel like my family would be better off without my bad decisions.)

My failures became my identity. One catastrophe after another circled like a pack of wild animals, waiting to make their final pounce. Broke, barely "making it" through a work day, and unable to control my emotions, I couldn't see the opportunities in front of me, nor could I see my own capabilities. I spent far too many of my days with a puffy red face from ugly crying over wine and salty chips.

I wonder, sister, if you've been there. Have you ever cried out in pain when life seemed to be too much? Have you ever broken apart and desperately tried to stitch yourself back together like Sally from the *Nightmare Before Christmas*, only to have your seams pop every time you move? Have you ever been lost and frustrated, going through the motions of life because you can't see the way out of your messy world?

Not one to quit, when I found myself in this dark place, I resolved to dig in to give it my absolute best try. Everything seemed to get worse, and I unintentionally collected a series of curse words I adopted as my own. I let them identify me, bully me, curse me.

I kept going, but I was always "too tired." I did the work but complained of being "overwhelmed" by my responsibilities. I "always" had to give all of myself to everyone else and "never" got to relax.

Each one of these words chipped away at who I really was until I became aware and found a solution. I realized these labels no longer served me and I found solutions to wake up from them and start pursuing a better way, an easier and smarter way.

I discovered how to let it all go and walk directly into something different, and it was fucking magical. In unusual ways, I flipped the switch of these curse words and started using them for fun again. I took my curse words and taught them a lesson. I picked up my paddle and swung, shattering open the confining characteristics of my life until all that was left was love, fun, and renewed passion.

How would it feel to take your curse words and beat them open with a paddle until all that's left is love, and fun, and renewed passion?

I did it the hard way. Let me help you find the easy way.

I'm thrilled to share the unusual, sometimes odd solutions that helped me pull my curse words out at the root. I'm still a hot mess of a work in progress, but I own my awesomeness, love my life, and have found fulfillment and peace in these simple switches.

What are your curse words?

Life moves in heartbeats.

Sometimes, lives don't change until the heart of another stops beating. Other times, it's in the rhythm-skipping utterance of words like "I do" or "It's over."

But the big stuff for the average human, the milestones of life we benchmark our journeys by, usually come after long periods of waiting followed by a whirlwind of commotion. Then, it's over, and our days readjust to normal. We sit, perched on the edge of our seats, waiting for the next life-changing moment so we can feel new and alive and hopeful again.

Those moments dictate who we are and how we feel, and we wait for the "good times" because they help us believe we're "doing it right." The graduation caps tossed into the air, the man on one knee, and watching our children say the word "shit" to a stranger for the first time (yes, I think that's magical... well, at least the look on the stranger's face is), become the only things worth remembering. Then we get hit with a foreclosure or bankruptcy, we go through divorce or collapse from the loss of a loved one.

We get to experience some of the greatest highs in life, as well as suffer through the worst lows. And every time we go through the hard crap, we should remember the good stuff, right? What happens when we can't? When the heartbeats of life—the day-to-day moments that add up and contribute to our earthly existence—become less important because we can't stop focusing on our nostalgia for the good moments or the pain of the bad, we miss out on so much.

If we aren't careful and diligent about the way we live, we end up measuring our lives by the very best moments and the very worst. It's all either "amazing" or "devastating," and somewhere in there, we forget that every day is new.

What if there's more magic in life, and we just weren't trained to see it?

We all want to believe in magic, don't we? Stories entice us to look at the back of wardrobes to find a magic world, shake a bell between our fingers to hear the ringing that comes only to those who believe. Finding magic seems elusive and the stuff of stories, but what if you could write your own story and put the magic in however you wanted?

Magic, on its basic level, is the ability to instantly change a thing into something new. There are impractical rules of magic, like the kinds we find in fantasy books where a shoot of the wand can create a pig's tail on a victim. It's unlikely that we expect to be bestowed with that sort of supernatural wizardry, but there are ways we want to believe things can magically change.

The lottery.

Love at first sight.

A dream job falling at our feet.

Understanding quantum physics (It's fascinating and I try, but I just don't get it outside of watching *Nova* on PBS).

We want to believe in this practical magic so much that we chase it. But let's be real. If we caught it, we'd barely be able to hold onto it.

I cried out for magic last year, or at least a miracle. I prayed for my life to change when I was buried in work and getting stress-induced skin problems. That resulted in the use of more steroids than my body could handle, leading to heart issues I feared would make me see the light at the end of the tunnel, and not in a good way. Oh yeah, and then there were those pre-cancerous cells on my back that came from my immune system attacking itself. When I fought through the itchy pain and medication trials, I cried out for magic.

When my publishing company didn't have a solid marketing plan, and despite my best efforts sales fizzled before they ever sparked, I begged for magic. Miracles would make our books be magically attractive to millions of people once they knew we had access to nuggets of literary gold. When I wasn't profitable, I cried out for magic.

My family suffered from my workaholic, hamster-wheel-spinning of a schedule on the daily. If only I could make my seven, five, and two-year-old children understand why Mommy couldn't play. If my husband believed in my vision as much as I did. In my "if only," I cried out for magic.

And then I got it. I got my miracle. Oh, it came disguised as a breakdown, but I got it. I cleared myself of stress, turned my company around, and fixed my family and marriage. I did it very quickly—from a bird's eye view, one might even say I did it instantly. Yeah, that's what I call magic.

I've since realized that all magic really is, is the ability to make significant changes in minimal time. And guess what, chicken butt? You have that ability too. That's right. You're magic.

Let that sink in: you, my sister, are fucking magic.

If you desire change and allow for it to happen, you can make even the largest alterations happen in a hot New York minute. Magic is a flipped switch, a disappearing act, and an open door, but most of all it's the *choice*.

You have the ability to radically reposition yourself into an endless number of possible lives, but perhaps you choose not to recognize the power within you, and so you collapse infinite potentials. By allowing, accepting, and embracing the movement of change—despite discomfort and fear—you can live fully in the identity you were created to live in.

"What the hell does that mean?" you ask.

(I'm so glad you asked. Really. I wouldn't have been able to say this next part, and I worked really hard to craft it. Let me clear my throat…)

It means you can live up to your fullest potential.

("Oh goodie, she said the typical high school graduation thing everyone's heard a hundred times." Stick with me.)

You can wake up and say, "This is a bullshit life I've created for myself. It's time to roll out of this bitch and into my best self."

Our brains are an amazing, yet really complicated, filing system for past experiences and emotions. If, for instance, you've never had a successful date and have been rejected by every person you've even remotely liked, you might adopt those experiences as your identity and decide being single must be "just who you were meant to be." Before you start cry-grumbling when another one of your friends gets engaged and refuse to go to the wedding, consider that you might be holding yourself back due to a false belief.

It's pretty cool how our brains work—maybe I'm the only one who finds neurological studies fascinating, but I bet I'm not. Our brains fire and wire in patterns that "help keep us safe." As impressive as these biological mechanisms are, they run our lives, often driving us into ruts we don't want to be in (we'll talk more about that later). Our brains are great, but they will never be able to change our minds.

And if nothing changes, nothing changes.

To have something new in life, you need to *try* something new, and your brain will throw every single trick out the ol' top hat to keep you from experiencing the unknown. It's because we're biological creatures who are still trying to protect ourselves from lions, and good luck telling your brain that you live in a society where lions aren't a problem. To the brain, everything is a lion waiting to eat you.

That's where your heart comes in. If you want something new and set out to discover what the emotions are behind having it, your heart will push you forward even with that lion stalking you in the bushes.

What was once a struggle, isn't. Our minds are changed, not as a result of our brains, but because of our hearts. And when the two work together, you can do anything. *Anything.*

Instead of waiting for magic to happen *to you,* what if you could create that magic for yourself?

I did it. I made magic for myself, and I'll show you how I turned self-created roadblocks (fear, stress, overwhelm, loneliness, and more) from ruining my life into easily-conquerable challenges. I took all of my "curse words"—my overwhelm, my worthlessness, my fragile pain—and overthrew them. Sometimes I neutralized the curse word with a flood of the opposite emotion; other times I ditched them in favor of new (effective) ways of handling life. And some, I fixed with straight-up ridiculousness.

Whether you're lost, hurting, sad, or overwhelmed, you can turn your curse words around, too. And with the right tools, you can do it almost instantly. You can find the things in life you want, solve problems you never thought you could tackle, reach your goals without going insane or flopping your exhausted body over the finish line.

You can change your life into something so incredible that you wake up screaming, "Yeah bitches. Let's DO THIS!"

You don't have to be stressed anymore, or overwhelmed, or exhausted. You no longer need to be defined by "always" and "never," but can boldly step into a new reality. And although the long-term changes don't happen overnight, you can flip the switch straightaway.

You have that power within you. You were created by the Divine to be a creator, and with that ability, you can create the life you've always wanted. You can take those words that have "cursed" you and use them to your advantage by finding unusual solutions.

You, sister, can be the person you were meant to be and do the things your heart craves.

You. Now.

See? I told you you're magic.

WORTHLESS Piece of Shit

Holy mother of everything that sucks balls; some days are terrifyingly awful.

Do you ever wake up (rudely, either from a cat walking on your face or a child screaming that they spilled a whole gallon of milk), and somewhere in the space before your eyes open you wonder if you have any value left? Like, if someone put all your talents, skills, and services up for auction, you might get a final whopping bid of a Ritz cracker in exchange for everything you've worked so hard to build? It happens all at once, amiright?

Your boss returns that project you worked on for weeks, saying it needs a major overhaul by tomorrow. Your daughter's teacher calls because her shoes are too tight. The whole "Put on your shoes. Why aren't your shoes on yet? Just put on some shoes so we aren't late for the eighteenth time this semester!" routine from this morning flashes before your eyes. Now her toes are squished into a pair of shoes you forgot to take to Goodwill, and the teacher asks in her sweetest, most concerned voice, "Do you have enough resources to purchase new shoes, or would you like me to get you in touch with our financial aid counselor for substantive funding?"

Insert blank stare and internal screaming.

Then—because it always happens like this—you run into your ex or that coworker you never can seem to impress at the store while you're covered in dog vomit (don't ask), and they look like they just finished a restful vacation and are on their way to a party with Lebron James. You have diapers and a cucumber in the cart because that's all you could remember was on your list.

Whatever you do, don't go opening your Instagram or browsing through Pinterest. You'll only feel worse.

These days are so appalling because everything compounds, flooding out all the good bits of our lives. Our troubles fill our minds with the numbing feeling that no matter how hard we work, no matter what our focus, and no matter how much bullshit we shovel through to get to the glorious love of life, we still come out worthless.

I've experienced years' worth of these days. Sure, every few days went off without a hitch (miraculously, and usually because I didn't leave the house). But the bad ones magnified the gnawing at my self-worth causing an avalanche of self-doubt. I fell behind on most deadlines—usually self-inflicted ones—and then tried to overcompensate by making elaborate promises. Trying to make up for my failings, I only succeeded in setting myself up to fall short again.

"I'll have that assignment done and turned in tomorrow," I regularly said to my day job boss. "Next week it'll be two days early, I promise. Please don't fire me. *Ha-ha-ha.*" I gobbled up blame and never took any of the credit.

Owning and operating a start-up business on top of it all hasn't necessarily "helped."

Sure, I've done amazing things in the last two years. I've gained enough education and skills to get myself a well-paying day job. I've built a company with a beautiful reputation, publishing multiple authors and building a team of editors, designers, and marketers with whom to back up this dream. Sure, I have a great title as Owner and Editorial Director of Filles Vertes Publishing (that I worked my tail off to create for myself). I even have the business cards to prove it.

I'm going to be honest here because as a reader that's what you deserve; I also hadn't made any money. Like… none. I've paid myself a few hundred dollars. Everyone else came first. I invested my profits and income back into my start-up company, and I'm extremely blessed to have the ability to do that. I committed to reinvesting profits back into the company until I hit a certain level of success. But instead of focusing on that blessing and patting myself on the back for keeping my commitment and not giving up, I've thrown the world's longest pity party about it all.

Let me tell you a secret: I started this company, originally, only to publish my work. I figured I'd open a small press and invite others to join in. The whole thing took off faster than a granny on a jet-powered scooter. I got sucked into the beauty of manuscripts being submitted to me and abandoned my dreams in favor of theirs. And yeah, I've had bitter moments in the last few years while I helped build platforms, publish, and sell the dreams-do-come-true for others. I don't regret a step of it—not one. I've helped bring beautiful books to fruition, but I wish I hadn't spent so much time wishing my writing was "ready" like theirs.

From the outside, I was making progress—publishing award-winning books, keeping up with my day job (which I have the added blessing of enjoying and being able to do from home), and keeping my family together in a social-media-worthy way.

Nothing was working on the inside. I craved the peaceful confidence I saw in other female business owners, but finding it was like grasping at the air.

I simply couldn't do it all. I couldn't have my job, run a company successfully, be a good mom, support my husband in his high-stress job the way he supported me in mine, volunteer at the church, keep up with my friendships, keep my dreams alive, support my sisters and parents, eat healthy, and not die of dehydration, all while smiling. Forget all the extras of life like enjoying holidays. I stayed up so late on Christmas Eve once answering emails that the joy on my kids' faces the next morning barely registered for me. Milestones like the tooth fairy visits and pumpkin carving had become very fuzzy memories amid the haze of my full, overworked, curse of a brain.

Each time I failed to "be there" for my family I felt like a worthless mom and wife. When I sat down to work on my own writing, I couldn't get over the rejections that plagued me, until eventually, I gave up. Generating sales reports for my publishing company made me want to quit. Once I gained ten pounds, I shamefully covered up, assuming I wasn't worthy to be looked at. I stopped inviting people over to my house because who wanted to walk through piles of garbage just to have coffee at a sticky, work-splattered table?

I craved a life full of creativity and simplicity, but only overwhelm, chaos, and worthlessness orbited me. And that was the problem. I was focusing on "not losing" and "not being worthless" instead of focusing on winning and my *true* value.

I look back over the last 24 months and now see the chaotic beauty of it all. Amid the seemingly never-ending storm, there were many successes. Even though waves crashed all around me, I weathered them and grew stronger and more knowledgeable. Even though the rain of my own design pelted me in the face, I kept building my raft. Remember, I was determined to sail. I set sail many-a-time only to get swallowed by the next torrential wave only to regroup on the beach once more. At least I never mucked up anything in an irreversible way; I was always ready to rebuild. If my raft didn't work, I'd build a dingy. When that failed, I opted for a sailboat. Each time, I crashed against the shore until I found a "working vehicle."

And you know something about building the right vessel over years? I also learned how to become the captain of it; I figured out *how* to sail, too.

I now have a company that is well on its way to "thriving." I did that (with help). *Me.*

The thing is, I spent years looking through such a negative lens that I didn't see those tiny moments of beauty as they happened. I didn't see that I was saved from drowning in my dingy or how the supplies to rebuild just kept "mysteriously" appearing. I couldn't see the blessings; I only saw the fact that I couldn't get off the beach. If you've ever started a new job, started a business, gained a new spouse, or had a child, you know that all the little moments of joy are often smothered by learning curves, diapers, and fights.

Feeling good about yourself while it's happening seems impossible.

It's hard to believe you're deserving when you're broke, don't look the way you wish you did, feel stupid, work without reward, and feel like everyone is just tolerating you and secretly hates you. Show me someone who feels any of that *and* feels worthy of an abundant life and I'll introduce you to their pet unicorn who won't get off the Leprechaun-spun, golden covers.

How do we overcome all the bullshit we believe about ourselves and create this worthy person we were meant to be?

First, you don't. Sorry. I'm sure it's a real bummer to have the first instructional piece of advice be "you can't do that." You really can't make yourself worth more.

You already are worthy. You can nurture pieces of yourself to become smarter, richer, thinner/thicker, more creative, whatever you want, but you cannot make yourself worthier.

Because, honestly, you're already there.

But—like a brontosaurus, there's always a sizable but—you can change the way you and those around you see your worth, and that's where we'll focus. I don't want to change *you*; I want to help you change the way you see yourself.

Put on the Crown, Even if it's Uncomfortable to Wear

I tried to be graceful as a teen and young adult (if you know me, please don't snort; no one here knows how ridiculous that statement is). So, even though I held myself to the highest visual standard, always keeping myself in peak condition (I said stop laughing), I've recently discovered a physical abnormality in which my shoulders want to fall forward instead of resting gracefully back.

Yeah, I have bad posture. Maybe it's from all my time spent working in front of a computer, or I could blame it on carrying three babies to full term and then carrying them on my hip for years. Or, I could put responsibility where it's due and admit I never had great posture to begin with.

Over the years, it's only gotten worse. Sometimes the strain in the triangle between my shoulder blades and the base of my neck makes tears push their way out of my eyes. I can see a lump in my upper back forming—albeit a small one—when I let my body collapse forward in exhaustion. I'm not a fan, and since I'm only 5 foot 2, I can't afford to lose an inch from bad posture, nor do I care to pop acetaminophen for the pain.

As soon as I became aware of this habit and had a reason to change, I resolved to fix my posture. I learned exactly how to settle my body into a correct stance (apparently, you want to stand against the wall feeling your heels, upper buttocks, and shoulders make wall contact). I practiced and adjusted every time I thought about it, and I started to see improvement even when old habits crept in. For the most part, I "fixed" my posture.

Except, you know what I figured out about "fixing" the way I held myself? Let's review the following list:

I traded my upper back strain for mid and lower back pain as my muscles readjusted to the new position.

It was hard to remember to do it. To break any habit, one must form a plan to replace that bad habit with a new one (standing up straight instead of slouching), and one must constantly remind one's self to do said new habit with near-obsession to make it stick. Then again, "they" say a habit only takes 10-30 consecutive days to make, so it isn't supposed to take forever.

And, it was uncomfortable. I mean, let's embrace the awkwardness of this and call it what it is; I felt like I was walking around stickin' my boobs out.

The last part, to me, has been the worst. I like my chest all right but showcasing it felt ridiculous and unnecessary. I found that in some moments, literally, any time someone looked my way, I wanted to retreat into the c-curve of a spine I've been used to. I would rather slink back into the old version of myself—a version that, by the way, never served me or made me feel good—than have someone think I was trying to thrust out my boobs.

Emerging from the pain of my worthlessness and into the beauty of how *worthy* I truly am felt the same. It was like walking around, sticking my "goods" out for everyone to gawk at.

"Look at me!" I felt like I was saying with my new positive attitude. "I'm the *best*. I'm not saying y'all should bow, but some rose petals thrown at my feet would be nice."

I'm not a showboaty person, to begin with; most people who struggle with worthlessness aren't. I often came across that way, especially to those close to me. My lifelong insecurities made me feel like I constantly had to prove myself, which was often construed as awkwardness, bitchiness, or being a "show off." Proving myself almost always backfired, and I felt worse.

I convinced myself for years that I was "shy," when what I really lacked was the understanding of my self-worth. I wanted to be confident, but I felt weird in a painfully awkward way. Could be weird in my *best* way?

I just wanted to fit in so bad that I let who I truly was slip away.

That's what worthlessness does; with value set at zero, the ability to embrace one's true self is nonexistent. We are living instead by unattainable standards that chip away at true identity. When we care more about what others think about us than what *we* think about *ourselves*, we're creating a recipe for pain. All the world is a number's game, and statistics back everything. A percentage of the people you meet aren't going to like you anyway; that's a guarantee. You must ultimately decide if your self-worth is worth the expense of trying to please others more than pleasing yourself.

When I began embracing the "messy" bits of my personality, I fell into a rhythm with my soul. It didn't feel comfortable at first. It felt like I was "stickin' out my boobs." But I leaned into that discomfort—still do—and I work to let go of what others think. We don't like being uncomfortable, do we? Sometimes it's exactly what we need though, even if we think we aren't ready for the new.

My brain wanted to keep me safe from the "lions" by telling me that if I straightened my back—something that is undeniably good for my muscular structure and beneficial in the long-haul of life—the "lion" of someone accusing me of sticking out my boobs would eat me alive. The horror. I had moments where I'd see that lion and retreat, but I always found that giving up didn't make me feel good either, so out I thrust my boobs.

What others think is none of my business, anyway. Instead of the worry and tension and strain that comes from unmet expectations, I chose to let go of the opinions of others and just "do me." When "you do you," you can be exactly what the Divine created you to be: *you*.

And *you* are worthy and beautiful and complete from the inside out. You can be enough for today and have the strength and wisdom to grow to be the best *you* tomorrow. With God in you—the Divine in you (isn't that name delicious?)—you can live the best life you can possibly craft, something you can't do if your focus is on others and all the things you *aren't*. You don't have to *do* anything to be worthy of a good life; you just *are* worthy of a good life.

Perspective

If we can't change the way others see us, then what can we change?

Do me a favor; curl your hand into a thumbs up symbol. Now, close one eye and hover your thumb about ten inches away from the subtitle above. On the count of three, switch your eyes, so the opposite one is open, and the now open one is closed.

One, two, three... perspective.

Somewhere along my journey, I believed the story I told myself. You know what I mean; there's the truth about what happened in every situation we've ever experienced, and then there's the "truth" of what we believe about the situation.

It was easier for me to believe the story that no one cared about my work, the books I'd worked so hard to produce in my company, than the truth. The truth was, I sucked at marketing. Instead of realizing that I had a hole in my business and concentrating my efforts to fix said hole, I decided to perpetuate the lie that nobody cared.

We believe the stories we tell ourselves and walk around waiting for someone to tell us we're worthy of something. We wait to get promoted to feel worthy of our job. We wait to get engaged to feel worthy of love. We wait until our kids start getting awards in school before we feel worthy as a parent.

You know what this misguided perspective does? It gives everyone around us the power.

Overcoming "worthlessness" doesn't require an outward action. Instead, it comes from an idea shift. Where I once struggled to understand why no one cared enough to buy my books, I've since decided to focus on quality marketing campaigns to be distributed to a large portion of the "right" clientele. Instead of making my message perfect, I decided to do the best I could and just be myself, letting those who are attracted to my message invest in it. I've also hired out expert help and am able to be the thought leader behind the direction I send my team in. We must reprogram our ideas about ourselves, and this process takes time and feels weird.

If you're looking for outside validation of your worthiness, not only may you never get it, but if you do, it won't feel real. If you don't change your mental narrative, it doesn't matter if you get that job, spouse, child, body, achievement, or thing you've always wanted—you'll feel the same way you do now. If your mental narrative says, "I've fucked up in the past and I'm just certain I'll do it again," or, "I might as well bow down to my circumstances and my painful past," then you will never be able to fully appreciate the gifts you've been given or find your worth.

I don't know about you, but I want a peaceful confidence that isn't dependent on my past or my current circumstances.

"But outside opinions are everywhere!"

They are.

"But our culture is so mean."

I know.

"But I was conditioned to hate myself."

Me too.

"But my past is too awful. I'm a victim and will never feel worthy."

Let me introduce you any of the people who populate when you type, "Celebrities who lived through horrible childhoods to create success" (*cough Oprah Winfrey*) and the countless others who are and aren't in the media who have suffered unimaginable abuse and rose above it to live fulfilled and purpose-driven lives.

"But I can't just turn on a dime and love myself."

Yes, you can.

"But I've hated myself for so long."

I did too.

I love you, sister (whoever you are), and so I'm going to say the thing your friends won't say to you. Take a deep breath and make sure you're sitting for this one…

You have made your *excuse* more important than *you*.

I'll give you a minute to go get some ice for that sting.

If you don't let go of the excuses you've made for why you aren't good enough, you will waste your life and sacrifice endless opportunities. I don't mean to be insensitive. Poverty, illness, rape and sexual abuse, violence, and drug addiction; these are all heinous parts of life. You may be in a situation where looking at yourself in the mirror and repeating a mantra of "I'm worthy" may be all you can do. It may not seem to do anything at first.

But this is where your perspective comes in.

Are you alive? Then keep breathing.

Can you move? Then keep going.

Have you ever supported yourself? Then you could do it again.

Can you read? Then keep learning.

Keep going, sister.

Boundaries

Being a mom, I've seen some of the fundamental boundaries of life get thrown epically out the window. Like peeing in privacy? Changing without having my two-year-old sneak in and point to my butt with cheeky laughter (pun intended)? Oh lord, I've even had my girls pick the bathroom lock and continue their living room fight over who got to color the specific page in the coloring book at the side of my *bath*.

Sometimes, we have to bend our boundaries. Most of the time, we don't.

The gal in the cubicle next to you doesn't have to dump her boyfriend drama on you every day at lunch. You get to draw a boundary and tell her you are spending your time differently. It's okay to pat her on the shoulder and tell her you're there for her without letting her drain you.

If you accidentally offend someone, it's okay to assess the situation and apologize and adjust your behavior without having that person walk all over you because you said one hurtful thing. Be your best moving forward and draw a boundary, so they don't make you relive your bad mistake over and over—spouses, I'm talking to you.

And yeah, if you need an uninterrupted bath, draw the boundary with your kids: "If mommy's in the bathroom with music on, that is your cue to go get daddy."

As we grow and discover our worth, it gets easier to set boundaries.

You no longer need to plant yourself in someone else's garden and let their opinion be the root of how you feel. Instead, change the dirt around you by "replanting" elsewhere. This doesn't mean you're always going to be able to ditch your problems and the people in your life whose opinions you don't like. But sometimes it does.

The reality is, those of us who aren't sociopathic are empathic on one level or another. All this means is we can identify with another person; we can feel what they might be feeling or think about what they may be thinking about. Let's not get caught up on labels here; some of us are more sensitive to feeling or connecting with people than others, but we all feel the energies of others in one way or another. While this can often be pleasant, it is more often draining and contributes to our self-worth. Just because we feel the feelings of others or understand what they might be thinking doesn't mean it should hinder us in any way.

Don't allow the feelings and thoughts of another person affect your feelings and thoughts and make you feel worthless. Set some boundaries.

How do we do that? How do we make the thing we want to protect sacred enough to have a boundary around it? This will look different for everyone, but the principle is the same; draw a circle around it.

If you're a mom who feels worthless when every time you want to do something for yourself, you are interrupted, then set aside a specific time in the day to work on your wants and set boundaries around it. Maybe you need some self-care in the form of a bath, like I do. Maybe you need to go for a run or enjoy a meditation session, but your kids have never-ending school projects, and your husband announces that he agreed to go golfing with his coworkers. Instead of always complying, schedule the time you need and draw a circle around it. It's okay to tell your kids you'll help them after you've filled your own cup, even if they don't fully understand. We want to model good behavior for them, so they don't grow up with the same feelings of worthlessness, too. It's okay to stand up for yourself and discuss with your spouse that you need time, too.

Boundaries are critical for self-protection. If you need thirty minutes of silence to start your day, get up thirty minutes earlier and lock yourself in a quiet room so no one can interrupt. If you have a friend who makes you feel like a hot pile of garbage, establish what you will and won't put up with (or critically decide if you want that person in your life anymore).

Because—and hold onto your knickers for this one—if you don't set boundaries for yourself, no one else will either. You'll find yourself walked on more times than not. Even if someone doesn't intend to hurt you (your kids, for instance) that doesn't always mean they're going to take proactive steps to ensure you're feeling worthy and fulfilled.

Only you can set boundaries, and through them, you can find true security.

Go Simple

I overcompensate; it's what I do when I fail. And giving up the need to overcompensate has been a huge challenge for me.

I'm already the type of person who expects a lot out of myself. So, when it comes to making promises, I tend to overestimate myself and my abilities just enough that I feel like I always fall short. Oh, this has hurt me. I have promised so many hang out sessions that I'd end up canceling on because I also over-promised with work. Instead of being 110% there for work and 120% there for my friends and family, I was, like 30% there for each, leaving everyone feeling shortchanged. I thought everyone saw how overbooked I was from every angle. But their disappointment in my lack carved into my identity. Instead of just promising less, I decided I was a "fuck up."

The resulting disappointments hardened into worthlessness and defensiveness.

My husband got used to this by teasing me. "I'll be ready in 10 minutes" statements meant he had at least an hour to mow the lawn and shower before I reached for my purse. My boss stopped giving me projects that could've bolstered my position within the company because he couldn't trust that I would have them completed and turned in on time. I became an unreliable leader to my publishing crew as I continually fell short of my unbelievable promises. Even my kids put up with their fair share of broken promises. There's only so many times a kid can get excited for a museum visit only to have Mommy say, "Sorry, kiddos. I still have work to do, and we don't have any time left over." I'd see the hurt on their faces and beat myself up more.

If I could just be perfect, I often thought. *If I could just have it all together, if I could just do what I say I'm going to do then life would be so much better.*

The weight of my lack pushed me into bed early and kept me there late into the morning. It made me reach for the wine bottle almost as soon as the coffee was gone. I wanted so badly to prove I could do it all that I refused to let others help me, opted to take on extra work so my staff wouldn't have to, and lived chronically exhausted and resentful. And no one even said "thank you" for the things I did. Couldn't they see how hard I was working?

I hung up my entire identity on what I could and could not accomplish.

If you're doing that, I have the very best news for you. You can drop the weight. All of it. It won't be easy to pry it from your white-knuckled-hands—it hasn't been easy for me—but dropping the weight of expectations can be one of the most liberating experiences you will have. Sometimes, the best joys in life don't come from the next best thing, triumph, or bragging rights. Sometimes, the moments of greatest joy are found in the release.

Once you've dropped all the expectations and decided you're worthy enough without them, then you can pick back up only the things that fulfill you and lead to your purpose. You may stumble a bit and pick back up the wrong things or find yourself overcommitting again (if you're anything like me), but it's a dance you can master over time. Trust yourself enough to learn from your experiences and have the intuitions to know if something is too much for you to handle.

I am *not* saying "don't take on more than you can handle." That belief can be severely limiting and keep us from our purpose. But being chronically overwhelmed by your life doesn't help and is the more difficult side of the spectrum in which to find yourself dwelling. You can try new things, push yourself, and commit before you're 100% positive if something will work out or not. If you find yourself overwhelmed and misplacing your worth into the result of those actions, it's time to pull away and simplify.

You have your whole life to accomplish everything you want to do. You can take some time for yourself to feel truly fulfilled within the moment, and you don't have to dogpile every goal, accomplishment, and benchmark into one day and then feel worthless when you can't get it all done.

Simplifying also means you can find joy in one area of your life while a separate area falls apart. Just because one area of your life isn't working doesn't mean your entire life is awful. It's okay to put up your hands in surrender sometimes and say, "Look, this area of my life is a struggle right now, but I'm not going to stop being joyful in all other areas of my life because of it."

It's okay if you have an extra forty pounds around your midsection; just don't identify yourself as "undesirable" and cover up your body in layers of sweatshirts until your spouse categorizes you in the R2D2 grouping of unsexy. A struggle at work shouldn't mean you also beat yourself up as a mom and let yourself get so out of balance that you don't take time out for your kids. And just because you didn't finish that goal of yours in the time allotted doesn't mean you give it up entirely and classify yourself as a failure.

You can simplify and continue to find joy until you feel worthy of the life you live. Sister, you are worthy of it and more.

Change comes in baby steps, especially when it comes to the way you see your life and find your worth in all areas. Sometimes you'll shuffle forward and feel super positive and worth it, and other times, you'll backpedal. It's okay; give yourself grace or others won't be as inclined to show it.

Another zinger—sorry, not sorry.

DISAPPOINTED
Well, Fuck it

I went to college for performing arts.

Well, that's a lie. I went, originally, for a boy whose name I won't share.

As a high school senior who was deeply "in love," I applied for the same college as my boyfriend. Surely, I wasn't the only person in the history of girls and boys following the "love of their youth" to school. Except I only liked the guy because I starred opposite him in a Rodgers and Hammerstein production of *Cinderella*—which isn't a significant enough reason to follow anyone anywhere.

Oh yeah, the college was six states away. It was cute, it was a little rebellious, and it met my desires to travel as much as I figured I could.

Then, I got dumped. He dumped me hard—right after prom like a monster—by using the old, "Do you ever find yourself liking other people?" line of life-shattering bologna. It was too late, I had already been accepted and begun admissions process. I was committed and now met with a new responsibility: making it look like this was still my choice.

I suppose I could still be pissed at this little fucker, and I was for a long time. But I made the most of it, acting like staying at that college was my first choice anyway (it wasn't), and that I was there for the "renowned" theatre program (it wasn't), and that I didn't mind blowing 32 grand per year for two years until I came to my senses (girl, don't make me say it).

It took two years, multiple denied auditions, an unsuccessful try at being a lighting and sound tech, a mildly-successful attempt at being a stage manager, too many parties where I felt like an outsider, and a final decision that I was wasting my life (and money) before I quit.

I don't regret dropping out of college, especially since I was never passionate about theatre and because I'm still paying off those loans, so heaven forbid I doubled that amount by forcing the finish. I don't even regret going in the first place. It was under poorly-executed circumstances, but I had an overall great experience that I look back on fondly.

I do regret one moment.

My college boyfriend was significantly different from my lanky, sleekly handsome, singing high school variety. This dude had dark chops, an affinity for not washing his patchouli-soaked Baja sweatshirt, and a name that made others mistake him for an amateur punk rocker. Let's call him "Spike." He had college dream boy written all over him. The mom in me wants to go back in time and show him how soap works, but at the time, his affinity for the depth of philosophy outweighed his funk. I "loved" this boy, even more than the first. We stayed up all night talking, went camping on spring break together, and he introduced me to *Rocky* (the movie). I got C's on exams due to him and all our late-night convos. Not really. Let's pretend that's why.

Spike was well-liked among a wide range of people and surprisingly brilliant. He had the type of endless mind that soaked up information and instantly took ownership, proclaiming the new knowledge as his own brilliant ideas. He sang words of activism and progress, predicting many of the cultural changes I've watched come true in the ten-plus years since we've seen each other.

Then, Spike's attitude became a fast problem. His ego was too big, his arrogance made him unapproachable, and he wouldn't stop buying and smoking bad cigars in the beer-can-lined common area, a violation that got him and his five roommates nearly kicked out of housing on several occasions. The final blow for this oddly fascinating relationship came the day after I had a new vision for my life.

As mentioned before, I fulfilled a tiny bit of my wanderlust by traveling such a distance for college in the first place. The culture was comfortably different but lacked the verve for which I hungered. The coffee shops were shaded by oaks instead of pines, but the culture was very much the same.

One night, I traveled to the nearest city of Chicago to watch a friend's friend perform as Lena Younger in a local production of *A Raisin in the Sun*. The group of us ate Ethiopian food with our bare hands, strolled the city in the glow of the orange midnight lights. I fell asleep in the attic of my friend's grandma's house on an old cot next to a triangle-shaped, stained glass window with a copy of E.E. Cummings collective poems resting on my chest while my friends piled on the floor and at my feet.

Bohemian bliss, right?

I drove back to college with my friends, swimming my hand out of the open window, watching the rolling hills of golden grains whizz past while Rosie Thomas sang her twangy, bluesy voice through the speakers. It was heaven on earth; Chicago, the culture, the risk and reward of stepping out of my comfort zone long enough to have a new experience.

I shared this life-altering episode with Spike, eager to relay my revelation that there is more life at our fingertips than we've ever imagined and how we can follow our passions into the unknown to discover a whole new life. It was one of the first times I had this monumental revelation at this level: born from a decision, fresh from a new experience, and ripe for the nurturing.

"I can be anything I want!" I proclaimed, my notions swirling with the incense that he burned.

His response was less than encouraging. A scoff, an eye-roll, and a heavy explanation about how the esoteric concept of the rapid rise in life was a romantic notion that would disappoint me over and over.

In short, he didn't believe I could be anything I wanted to be. And because he didn't believe it, I chose not to, too.

That's the moment I regret.

I had an experience that led me to a new belief, but instead of cherishing and sheltering that belief until it grew unshakable roots in my heart, I chose to share my nugget of a new dream with someone who I thought loved me as much as I loved him. I chose to accept the opinion of another person about my life as more important than my own opinion. I never pursued my dream of living alone in a big city, getting involved in local theatre, or routinely falling asleep in an attic with poetry dancing through my mind while horns and sirens blared from the nearby stained-glass window.

I had no idea how I to make that dream come true, but I could've figured it out along the way. I'm not even sure that would've fulfilled my life, but I should have tried it.

My story has a happy ending, so don't get your pitchforks out for me.

As disappointing as his attitude was toward my blossoming ambitions, the small voice inside knew I could pick myself up, and move along if I didn't like the situation I was in. It only took me moving across the country, chasing after an ex-boyfriend to find it.

I filed the paperwork to defer my education a few weeks later and never looked back. I left Spike, too, and never once regretted that decision. In hindsight, his limiting beliefs—masquerading as highly educated ones—only pulled me down. I'd grown a lot.

I was oh-for-two in the romance department, but one other thing happened around this time that molded my view of disappointment

The first time I auditioned for a show—another Rodgers and Hammerstein classic, *Carousel*—I was convinced I would make the cast. After all, I'd rocked the lead of a similar production not long before in my small hometown. I sang the hell out of yet another Rodgers and Hammerstein classic "Oh, What a Beautiful Mornin'" from *Oklahoma!* and nailed the callback with my sweet dance moves. It was sure going to be awkward when the rest of the theatre department had to face the disappointment of being cast below a newbie like myself. I could practically see my name on the playbill.

"Myra Green plays Julie Jordan in her epic theatrical debut!"

Except, I didn't get a starring role, didn't land a supporting role, and I wasn't an understudy. My name didn't even show up when casting was posted in the hall of the theatre department. The list was tacked to the bulletin board, and my name was not on it.

I got to participate. Oh yeah, baby. I did.

Fulfilling my duties in my employed roll in the lighting and sound department, my job for that show was to slip microphones into condoms and strap them to the dancing legs of the lead male actors. Without the little microphones that snaked up their leotards and hooked over their ears, the audience couldn't hear these men sing while dancing. The rubber kept the equipment dry from sweat, and the ribbed texture kept the whole ensemble from coming loose when they "double cabriole derrière"-d across stage. Convenient for them. The little sperm snatchers made my fingers smell like perma-latex. Totally glam, right? Except the department couldn't afford for each actor to have their own mic, and they needed to be switched several times throughout the production.

In case you've lost track of this tragic tale, the boy I followed from high school was one of the supporting dancers in the cast who sang during a few of the songs with a shared mic. So, I had to change the thigh-sweat-covered latex-condom-covered microphone from between my ex-boy-friend's inner thighs. "Break a leg" took on a whole new meaning.

Despite the hellish task, I didn't hate the experience. Why? Like most women who made it through disappointing things, I had a girlfriend who helped me see the positive side.

Zephyr was the kind of calm-yet-vivacious friend every college girl needs. I took the job as "condom-mic girl" not because I was forced to, but because Zephyr was on the cast and convinced me of how fun it would be to play cards in the green-room after performances. She made me feel included and helped me see the bright side. I became a team player, learned new skills, made friends, and got to see a brilliant performance a dozen times from the best seat in the house. And I got to touch a few muscular thighs in the process. Don't hate; it was awesome.

Theatre may never have turned into my full-time gig, even if I had made the cast of that show (or the other half-dozen attempts I gave acting). It was a stepping stone to my greater passion for storytelling through literature. In the end—and it's never the end, right?—I had a great experience. I lived a whole different life that molded me and planted seeds of artistic vision in my heart. I still sing and dance, just not on stage. I still tell stories, just not in the form of acting. I still work with production teams, just in a different capacity. And I still touch muscular male thighs, only they belong to my sexy husband, and the act doesn't involve sound amplification.

Disappointment is a part of life. It happens to everyone.

People make disappointing choices. Someone could leave you and screw everything up in your life; you could get dumped at a possible benchmark moment in your life. It could ruin you, or you could make the most of it.

You could find yourself disappointed by the opinions of others. People won't always believe in you, and some will downright tear you down. You choose to either believe them and stay under their feet or kick their opinions aside and rise into your truths.

And you may end up in a position in life that seems downright cruel. You may become the dog walker for someone who treated you like crap in high school. Let's hope you never have to strap microphone-filled-condoms to the ex-boyfriend who broke your heart after you committed to following him across the country to a school where you knew no one except him. The point is, you have choices to make when the situations of life don't go your way. Do you want to bitch and moan, throwing yourself a perpetual pity party? Or would you rather make the most of the situation you're in, regardless of the circumstances?

When we're so used to seeing the darkness of each situation, a little bit of light can go a long way. Can you really just "turn on the light switch" to see the possibilities in every situation? Of course, you can, and it boils down to one key point. Learn to deal with disappointment, and we can cut the bullshit that we'll "never get what we want."

I can tell you with certainty what the solution isn't. The opposite of disappointment isn't the fulfillment of your desire. If it were, it would be possible to fulfill your way to happiness, and we can't do that. You can't earn your way to a happy life because you won't always get what you want. I'll repeat myself in case you missed it above:

Disappointment is a part of life. It happens to everyone.

In case you haven't met, allow me to introduce you; Reader, this is Life. Life, this is Reader.

So, we don't always get our way. Some people take this and turn it into a propensity to want less, set the bar lower, and stop dreaming so much. Does this lead to less disappointment? Pardon me while I indulge in a deep, Santa Claus-like belly laugh. Have you ever met someone who has set the bar in life so damn low that it probably seems impossible to be disappointed, yet what do they face constantly? Yup, more disappointment. And the disappointment that comes from a low bar and unpursued dreams is the worst.

It is okay to want things; love, acceptance, new dreams, support, etc. It's our human desire to keep pursuing, wanting, striving. The Divine created us that way. But it was never guaranteed to happen without roadblocks, speed bumps, and the occasional collision.

The answer is love.

We must love; love the journey, love ourselves and the mistakes we make along the way. We must love ourselves enough to trust that we can make it through anything. We must love the experience enough to find it interesting. Not inherently good or bad—why do we put every circumstance of life into the "good" or "bad" categories? Just interesting. Do you know what happens when we look at situations through the lens of fascination? We see lessons, beauty, and learning.

Let's stop allowing outsider opinions, events we can't control, and personal disappointments define us. We must take back the ownership of our unique journeys, and that starts with love.

Let's talk about love, baby.

Love Yourself First:
Baby Don't Hurt Me

There's an interesting principle that may be common knowledge but isn't necessarily common practice: We cannot fully love others until we love ourselves. We've probably all heard this principle at least 3,592 times in our life in one form or another. How many of us truly practice it?

To embody this attitude, we must first truly understand it. Let's break it down.

The noun version of the word love is, by definition "an intense feeling of deep affection." And the verb is to feel, act, and show that love.

Let's say two people meet and have an instant connection. They feel something they can't explain, so they call it a "spark." An elevated emotion intensifies their experience, and they dive deeper into the character of the other, finding similarities, connections, relatable stories and ways they complement each other. They probably have comparable habits and experiences but are different enough to learn from each other in a complementary way. When they finally feel the "love," it seems like they've always felt that way and call it "love at first sight." I'm not saying this is always the case, that it's common, or even that this over-simplified Cliff Notes version of "fast love" takes validity and wonder away from the situation. If love is true and intense, what if it also needs to be known well? Deep love can't, by definition, be shallow either in feeling or in knowledge.

Show me people who love each other profoundly and I'll show you some shit they've gone through or know about each other.

If a person place or thing is only slightly known, we can like it, even desire it. We can love our friends, but we have that one friend we *love* love because we know the depths of each other's souls, right? Strong love requires more than a brief or shallow experience. This doesn't mean love can't be quick and magical, but I believe many of us are misguided about what being "in love" is.

Similarly, where I "loved" the boys of my youth, when hints of true self surfaced, the love faded. And that's okay; it's a part of the journey. Real love comes from knowing each other deeply—profoundly enough to understand all the bits of who another person is while still letting the love shine through.

The point is, love between people happens over time. Even new parents, who feel instant love for their child, grow a deeper and deeper love with every benchmark in that child's life. Feelings that are similar to love (admiration, commonality, desire) happen quickly, but can we all agree that "Oh my god, Becky, I love you saying Groot is your favorite Guardian of the Galaxy, because he's mine too," isn't the same as, "After 45 years, their love continued to blossom in a marriage that set an example for many."

So, if true love requires a depth of knowledge into character, let me ask you this: Whose character do you know best? The guy you've been dating for four months or your own? I hope you know your own character more, otherwise you're dealing with an extreme identity and possibly self-worth crisis.

We know ourselves best, but we place our love in others first, even though we don't know them as well. What we're saying by this is, "I love the unknown in you more than the certainty in me."

People Pleasers

When we put others ahead of ourselves in the love department we're saying our wants, desires, and feelings don't matter as much as theirs. Now, I'm not talking about a shallow piece of this pie like a husband who won't put his socks in the hamper, but rather next to the hamper because God forbid he move four inches to the right. On the daily, the wife bends down to correct his bad habit for him until a load of resentment builds up. Why is it more important to pick of Nick's socks for him? Huh, Nick? Huh? *Huh*?! If she added up all that time she spent bending over picking up socks throughout her lifetime, she could have fit in an extra bubble bath or two instead.

I'm not talking about that kind of "putting others before ourselves." I'm referring to the type of love that hurts you and drains you. I'm talking about the one-sided friendship that you've poured long hours on the phone into, the kind where you never get to pick what you're doing for outings, and their advice always trumps yours until you feel too drained to be excited to be together anymore. But you stay in the friendship anyway because you feel too guilty to leave.

Sometimes we spend the time getting to know someone deeply and better than we know ourselves. Perhaps we don't feel we're worth knowing, not worth falling in love with. However, our human nature is to love and so that love has got to go somewhere. It goes into someone, and there's none left for us. This is also described as being a "people pleaser."

Can I tell you a secret? That's a total misnomer. It shouldn't be "people pleaser," it should be "people manipulator" because what you're saying with this action of always putting the needs and desires of others above your own is that you have the power to manipulate the situation to produce the desired result—someone else's happiness and fulfillment.

If this is you, I'm not dogging your heart. You have great intentions, believing that if you pour yourself into someone else, they will one day return the favor. Except that doesn't always happen, and the unmet expectations will lead you to disappointment nine times out of ten.

If your relationship is based on your performance instead of the quality of your character, you've got some contemplation to do. If I hadn't been so worried about pleasing my high school boyfriend by following him six states away, I might have found a greater direction for my college life. If I hadn't let Spike's opinion of me become more important than my own, I may have moved to Chicago and been a bohemian poet, or whatever I might have become.

I could've searched deeper into my soul, into the parts of myself that I knew and loved, and I could've forged a path for myself, not trying to manipulate those in my life by making the decision I thought they wanted me to make. It didn't, after all, keep us together. Either time. Nope, people pleasing has rarely worked to my benefit, yet I did it unapologetically for years.

Instead of trying to manage the circumstances of others to make them happy, why don't we just do our best to follow our journey, trusting that the outcome will neither be "good" nor "bad," but that the outcome for all involved will be interesting, and that everyone involved is capable of managing their own emotions around that.

"I Can't Afford it"

Yes, I know I'm talking about loving yourself more than others, but sometimes people love things before themselves too. When we bypass people all together and go straight to stuff, we don't feel worthy of love either. Our sights have narrowed to include only our accomplishments, titles, or material things.

We become obsessed with having a Mercedes or binge-watching our favorite show. Yup, I'll be that blunt friend who tells you to stop letting another binge-watching marathon get in the way of pursuing your dreams. You don't need to eat eight seasons of TV shows like your destiny is tied to the finale. Do you really want to live your life fixated on a string of new show obsessions until you die? Or would you rather live your life?

Loving stuff, achievements, and accolades is not an inherently bad thing. These can be good for us, motivating us toward a more filling and enriched life. But loving these things more than loving yourself is dangerous. It creates a lack of depth and leads to misplaced focus. You can enjoy having these things, but never love them more than you love yourself.

There's a great quote I once heard that says, "If it costs you your peace then it's too expensive." You should apply it to loving yourself too. If the cost of something is your self-love, it isn't worth it. Never. Period. Nothing worth having in life will make you destroy yourself to get it. I've heard way too many miserable people lament about how they destroyed themselves to pursue something. And it always turns out that the thing is never fulfilling. It's okay to have growing pains, so long as we don't rip ourselves apart for a dream, person, or thing.

We say we "can't afford" stuff all the time. We can't afford that house we've always wanted to live in or car we've always wanted to drive, can't afford to take time off, can't afford to go skydiving because our insurance doesn't cover the resulting injuries.

Then, in the same breath, we allow ourselves to be crushed under the weight of situations and relationships that were never meant for us.

What if, instead of saying about the stuff in our lives, "I can't afford it," we start saying that about situations and people?

What if you said to that soul-sucking job, "Look. I'm sorry, but I love myself more when I'm not around you. I'm going to form a plan to do work I love and make money at it because I can no longer afford for my soul to get sucked out of me every day like this." Or, what if you address that regret from your past, saying, "Hi regret. I see you. I acknowledge you as part of my life. I will learn from you, but I can no longer afford to invest long term and must let you go. You have become too mentally expensive."

Stop deferring the love you should be showing yourself. Stop loving others, things, and situations more than you love yourself. Honor them as interesting and then choose to love you. Every time you put anything or anyone above loving yourself, you leave a greater internal deficit.

Who in their right mind would give all their money to another person, actively draining their finances into the hands of another without replenishing the supply? That would leave you broke and dumb. Yet we do it with our love. We give it all away and expect others to replenish our supply or expect things and accomplishments to show up as a steady form of emotional income, and that ain't always going to happen.

Share the Love

Have you ever heard the Sunday School song about the penny? Basically, if you squeeze a penny tight between your fingers, you basically have nothing. After all, money's only good if it's moving around. If you share it, spend it, or give it away, you'll get it back. You'll be in the "flow." It's a pretty cool investing principle to teach kids, but love is the true lesson in the lyrics. Give love away and you'll have much; squeeze it and refuse to give it away, and how much will you get?

So, what does reciprocated love do? It replenishes and multiplies. But you can't multiply what isn't there. Shared love between you and another person, you and your work, you and a goal, all lead to the fulfillment you seek. Let go of trying to manipulate the person, experience, or dream and open yourself to the wonder of opportunities that life brings and learn from them. Give your love to yourself first and then to the people and things that make it multiply.

Stop draining your love into others before loving yourself. Yes, love others and expect them to love you in return (well, some of them), but forgoodnesssakeimgoingtoshakeyousayingthis love yourself first.

Refrain from over-giving. Giving and receiving should be an equal balance. Instead, give in balanced amounts, always putting the oxygen mask on yourself before you assist others. You know what I mean; if you've ever flown, you've mostly ignored those flight attendant instructions about helping yourself first in an emergency before helping others. Why wait until your life has become an emergency before putting the oxygen mask on yourself? Start flooding your lungs with love for yourself and explore that.

Get to know yourself and fall in love with your character, ambitions, dreams, quirks, all that beauty. If you don't know and love those parts, someone else's love for those parts will never fill that hole entirely.

When you love yourself first and love the work you do for yourself and others, when you decide to view every situation as interesting instead of inherently "good" or "bad," you don't have to manipulate every situation and person in your life. You can just live and let the rest come back to you. Because it will. Fulfillment will reveal itself, accomplishments will happen, and the most beautiful moments will unfold before your eyes. You'll marvel at the wonder of how life weaves together like a precious, intricate tapestry and you'll marvel at your part in it—which will never be as big a part as you think.

It's a-okay to feel the emotion of disappointment when something doesn't turn out the way you wish it had. Acknowledge those feelings of disappointment and then look at the situation objectively and find the interesting bits. Whatever you do, don't believe you are a disappointment. There's no reason to take that feeling on as a part of your identity.

You have nothing to prove. When you love yourself first, you can give the best of yourself and watch the best come back to you.

Now, if that isn't the solution to disappointment, I don't know what is.

STUCK
Stubborn Shit

When our oldest daughter hovered around the age of two, one of her favorite words was "Stuck." Only, she said it more like, "Sh-tuck."

Everything was shtuck.

The doorknob was shtuck.

The soap was shtuck.

The cereal was shtuck to the edge of the bowl at 3:32 p.m. when I finally cleared the table.

To this day, whenever my husband or I hear that word, we say (usually in unison) "Shtuck."

But as funny as it is to hear a two-year-old girl say "Shtuck" in her angel voice, it is far from an angelic place to be.

Being shtuck… I mean *stuck* sucks. When you're aware of your stuckness, it blows, but it's even worse when you're ignorantly wedged into a state of limbo. You could be stuck, even if you think you're as loose as Elvis's famous hips during "I'm All Shook Up."

Perhaps you've been stuck for so long that it feels like your standard of living, your unspoken identity (hmm, sounds like a curse word to me). The limits under which you live feel so normal by now that you may not see that you could do with a little "dislodging" from between your rock and the hard place holding you captive.

Or look, maybe you're not stuck in any part of your life anywhere, and everything always moves in a steady flow. If that's you, I offer you a sincere round of applause. Really, good job, Karen. Your flexibility in life has served you well. I still think you should keep reading. You never know, maybe you've just never been stuck *yet*. I'm just looking out for you; trying to give you the tools you need if and when that ever happens. I'd hate to see one of my sisters be that piece of shtuck cereal on the edge of the bowl without realizing it.

A (True) Fable of Prunes

I notoriously push myself and fill my schedule, without blocking out free time for myself. Even when my intentions are good, I can shove myself right to the brink of illness if I don't slow down sometimes, but mostly this extra effort in the day-to-day results in feelings of weariness and fatigue.

It sounds like a typical mother's excuse—that I have no time for me. I recognize my need for down time and promise that I'm constantly trying to up my spa game. I sleep a solid seven, I put those little white strips on my nose that are supposed to pull out clogged pores which just ends up ripping out my hair, and I'll be damned if I don't get at least one yoga sesh in a week. But, from the moment I wake until the moment I crash with my fam at the end of the day, I'm basically sprinting.

I've grown to love it. I feed off the momentum, get a lot done, and I set a good example for my kids on what it means to follow your passions (I also show them how to have fun and rest; my house is no factory). So, when I crash, I crash. Maintaining maximum positivity and "high vibes" takes a ton of energy.

Anyhow, don't we all have that moment we don't have anything to say to anyone? When that feeling strikes, most people isolate in the bath, pop open a book or go for a walk alone. I, on the other hand, take the opposite approach and hang out in the hot tub at my gym with a bunch of strangers. I like pruning. What can I say? I live dangerously.

I usually love socializing, even if it's awkward and heavily chlorinated. I've always loved telling stories, and any set of willing ears is audience enough for me. But when I don't feel like talking, I *really* don't feel like talking. That's when the headphones come out, and the other day was no exception.

Picture it: Friday night, end of the work week, I was satisfied with my accomplishments as I slipped into the bubbling hot water, steam rose steadily into the 68-degree evening. The woodfired pizza restaurant across the street lent its swirls of woodsmoke and garlic to the air. I slid my back against the wet tile wall and let the jet blast out the tension between my shoulder blades from being glued to my computer all week. I reached for my buds, trying to decide whether to fill my ears with Foy Vance's "She Burns" or "Upbeat, Feel Good" when I heard a voice that was decisively not my favorite musician.

"Who's that?" asked the lady across from me.

I looked up from my phone to see her staring, and so I followed her gaze down to my sister's face, which is tattooed on my forearm.

"Is it you?" she asked the clarifying question before I could answer the first.

I shook my head. "My sister." I smiled before resuming my song selection. So that I didn't seem rude, I waited a sufficient amount of time before slipping my headphones back in.

"I just had surgery," she said, before I could snuggle the bud in my ear.

The conversation wasn't over, and I fought the urge to sigh and kept myself from immediately jumping out of the water, because no one should be in a communal pool of water with an open wound. Common courtesy, folks. Plus, that's really gross.

"Oh yeah?" I said with a clever balance of I'm-being-polite-but-am-not-up-for-talking undertones to my voice. "What kind?"

"Hip surgery."

I nodded, understanding now why she was standing with her hip at a 90-degree angle toward the jet.

"I'm only three months out," she said. "Recovery has been good except for this pressure on my sciatic nerve and the numbness on my thigh."

"It looks like the heat helps," I lightened my tone, seeing that this wouldn't be a brief conversation.

No, I didn't feel like talking. Yes, I have manners enough to pretend I do *until* I do. There's just no excuse for rudeness, no matter how tired I was. No matter how much I wanted to hear Foy's tangy, sultry Irish voice croon some delicious words into my ear, I could be a decent human being and give someone who seems lonely five minutes of my fucking day.

"The heat *does* help," she said, excited that I was now engaging. "It's hard, because as soon as I get out of the water, I feel all the pressure of my upper body again and that's when the nerve pain kicks in."

"That sucks," I said, and I meant it.

My grandmother had the same surgery a few years ago and still suffers from extreme nerve pain in her foot as a side effect.

I didn't tell the woman this, though. I let her continue on about her doctor; she couldn't remember if his name was Dr. McGuire or Dr. McGill, Dr. McGuiness or even Dr. McClain, but she was pretty determined to figure it out. She talked about how the scar tissue feels like an old zipper under her skin and how she probably had a long road ahead of her. She couldn't be older than 60, though she wore her age like a burden; slumped shoulders, wild hair crammed into a baseball cap, tight lips that didn't offer a smile.

When she was done with surgery stories, the woman pointed again to my arm. "Is your sister... um... still *with* us?"

I nodded. "Tara and I haven't lived in the same state for almost a decade. I miss her all the time, but this helps."

She smiled kindly.

My body has been half-covered in tattoos for almost 15 years, so I'm used to the questions. I used to approach the subject with a "back off, these are my business" policy, but that always left me feeling ashamed of the artwork, and I love each piece. Ignoring them is like ignoring a part of me. Not always wanting to reveal the intimate parts of myself, I've crafted simple responses to satisfy questioners without becoming vulnerable.

The lady—I never got her name—twisted her lips in the corner ever-so-slightly and I could tell she didn't quite approve of my ink. Thankfully, she chose to ask a less invasive question. "Where does your sister live?"

"Nevada."

"Oh no!" she nearly shouted.

My eyes widened, imagining the worst. I mean, I'm not the best for keeping up with the news until I hear it secondhand, so I figured I must have missed a shooting or freak weather pattern, or something.

"Why?" I leaned forward. "What happened?"

"Oh," she shook her head like she had some news to break to me. "That whole state is on a fault line that's going to break any minute. Forty-six inches of water is what they had down in South Carolina last week. Forty-*six*. That's taller than that fence right there. Imagine what will happen in Nevada when that fault line… oh, what's it called? The San Andrew? No, that's wrong, the San Antonia? No." (She was back to being hung up on names again.) "San… oh well, it's there. That fault line is going to snap, and all of California and Nevada are going to be devastated. Absolutely annihilated."

I clearly missed something on CNN (Facebook) about this and could feel my heart picking up speed. Were my sister and her family in danger? I knew tons of people in California. What would I do if they all suddenly weren't here because of a freak natural disaster?

Or… this wasn't actually a thing. Yep. That's it. This wasn't a thing.

Cue deep breath.

Don't get me wrong; I don't think the science behind this warning or any other is bogus. The study of fault lines, quakes, storms, tsunamis, weather patterns, and all that jazz is totally legit and very appreciated. But also, Yellowstone National Park is technically one massive volcano that could be more than six thousand times as big as Mount Saint Helens' explosion in 1980 that could *technically* be the end of civilization as we know it.[1] Technically.

Even though the headlines on such articles read, "Warning!" and "Doom is Imminent," experts insist there's only a 0.00014% chance of it happening. That's lower than the chance of an asteroid hitting Earth.[2] So, while it's possible, neither my sister nor I should live our days with a sense of doom.

Anyhow, while I was busy wondering if this lady was secretly harboring an apocalyptic shelter in her basement, she rambled on about flooding, earthquakes, devastation in Japan (I don't even know which year she was talking about, to be honest) and cycled all the way back to her hip. It was quite the journey, and thankfully, I didn't have to do much talking, after all. I just needed to nod politely until she decided she'd "have a heart attack from the heat" and needed to get out.

I wished her well on the rest of her recovery, watched her walk out of the tub as if she wasn't really in pain (I'm sure she was, but she carried herself well in the end), and I was once again alone.

By then, however, I didn't feel like listening to music anymore. Ironically, I felt like talking. I mean, this lady teased me with topics I could've participated in. I could've told her about my grandma's surgery and how much better off she was; at least she didn't have permanent damage that required special shoes. I could've told her that the chances of moderate to seismic earthquakes happening in Nevada are ever-looming, and how if it happens—shrug—it happens. We'll all probably be destroyed one of these days. Worrying about it only causes one to suffer more than necessary.

I could've said all this, but she didn't give me much room to interject (which was fine) and didn't seem like she would've been receptive anyway.

I spent five minutes with this lady and learned a very key piece of her personality; she was stuck in a mental loop. Without guidance and being open to change, she would probably always be stuck on the same negative cycle. The content may change, but she'd continue being sucked in a whirlpool of pessimism.

Thankfully, I didn't have to finish my hot tub experience in grumbling contemplation. As a yin to the last lady's yang, not a minute later, another woman of similar age occupied the same seat. She—I later learned her name was Vaughn—was a little older than the first and carried her age like a sweetness.

She offered me a sincere smile and said, "I was afraid it wouldn't be warm enough. This feels lovely."

"It does," I said. "Your *swimsuit* is lovely. The blue compliments your complexion."

She lit up at the compliment and patted a damp hand across her brow, smoothing her carefully braided white hair.

Because I'm an awkwardly quirky person (something I hope never to grow out of) I couldn't let the last thing I said be a compliment, so I started rambling about the weather, our national fallback topic of conversation.

"I like the hot tub best when there's a gentle snow that chills my shoulders," I said, because that's clearly what one says when working one's way out of weird, post-compliment energy.

"Me too," she replied with a reminiscent smile. "My favorite local column is by those two meteorologists, do you read it?"

I admitted I didn't, but my interest was piqued. Would she go the way of doom and warning or would she be bland? The suspense had me on the edge of my cement seat that had discolored and worn the butt of my suit.

"They were saying that we should have a white Christmas this year." (It was August.)

"Isn't that wonderful?" she beamed. "Fourth year in a row."

"Oh, a white Christmas is my favorite," I exclaimed, my voice filled with the same spirited excitement as if we were discussing Foy Vance and his sultry Irish voice... mmhmm. Anyways, sorry. The weather. I responded to her with more enthusiasm than I normally would because her smile was contagious.

For the rest of our chat, I noticed drastic differences in the two conversations.

"Ms. Doom," meet the clearly unstuck "Ms. Sunny Disposition."

Being stuck is more than a mind shift about the weather. We can find ourselves in a place, situation, or relationship that has stopped meeting our needs and is no longer fulfilling, yet we stay. Sometimes, our circumstances that make us feel "stuck" are unavoidable—sometimes we have to ride out a commitment until we've satisfied it or hang onto our lousy job for a few more weeks until our new one starts, because as much as we'd love to angry-quit, we've got bills, yo.

Outside circumstances can keep us stuck, and we'll tackle that and how to discern these times and what our purpose is in them. But what keeps us stuck, nine times out of ten, is our own negative thought patterns. And, as far as I've been able to figure out, unless we have an anxiety disorder, panic disorder, OCD or the like, we have control over our thought patterns.

Let me put this this way: if your brain has a clean bill of health, then it's your responsibility to captain it. Even if it doesn't—and this is coming from the source of my friends who battle with their mental health—it is still your job in life to do your best. Managing your thoughts during your most lucid moments earns you the right to ask for leniency when you are not capable of mental control. The point is to do the best you can with what you have. Period.

Yeah, I'm looking right at you. You can control your world by controlling your thoughts. If your brain is a wild monkey flinging its poo everywhere, how do you think your life is going to look? Or what if you let your brain become a sloth? You don't do anything to stimulate it, opting instead for mind-numbing activities that allow you to mentally "check out," and yet you wonder why your today is the same as your yesterday.

You're the keeper of your mind. You keep the sloth in check. You feed and entertain the monkey so it doesn't toss its shit.

What happens to a zoo when the zookeeper disappears? They hire a new one because otherwise, it's wild in there. And although "the wild" is great in the jungles of Central America, if you don't have control over the animals in your mind, it's going to be life-sucking chaos.

The point is, your mind is this beautiful, wonderful, deeply explorative part of you that needs attention.

Stuck vs. Seasons

Do yourself the biggest favor ever in the history of all of eternity and figure out the difference between what it's like to be in a "season" and what it's like to be "stuck." (I'm clearly passionate about this one.) Without knowing the difference, you run the risk of resisting all movement because you aren't clear of why you're being challenged. It isn't always our job fight our way out when life squeezes us; sometimes, we just need to keep marching.

Simply put, a season will unfold on its own accord, but getting unstuck results from steps that need to be endured.

Let's say you're standing in a valley with mountains towering over you from either side. It's hot here, and you're thirsty. Like, "Lord Jesus, I would risk the bacteria in that mud puddle if it could wet my whistle" thirsty. Your bottle of the good stuff is empty, and so you have three choices. Well, really two, because the first choice, always, is to do nothing. You could sit right there on your keister and let the dehydration slowly kill you, but that's not a viable choice. So, your *two* choices are to march forward, out of the valley where there's a lake, or to climb. The iodine tablets in your backpack will allow you to rest on the lakeshore with water-a-plenty. Those little vials of iodine hold, like, 18,452 tablets, so you'll be fine for a while before you must press forward. The lake seems a good option.

You begin to march forward when your boots crunch into the wet pebbles at the base of a glacial runoff. You trace the source, needing to put your hand over your forehead as a visor to squint from the sun's glare. At the top, a clean patch of glacier drips like an icy fountain at such a calm, steady rate that the water makes it all the way down here. Of course, down here, it's been mixed with bacteria and is no longer sterile enough to drink without treatment. It's also barely a trickle and you can't maneuver the spout of your water bottle to collect enough to warrant an iodine tablet anyway.

Sure, the water is still cool, and you wish you could slurp it right off the pebbles. But, everyone you've known who's done that has gotten severely ill from bacteria. If you want to make it out of this valley alive, you need water.

A "season" feels as though you're walking through the valley *en route* to the lake. You were meant to live on the shore, enjoy your time in the shade, and jump off your makeshift dock when you've grown warm from sunbathing. If your destination is a lake, you're in a season.

Being "stuck" is like walking through a valley, but the destination is the icy drip of endless glacial water. You were meant to be on the top, watching the eagles' backs as they soar, not their bellies. You were made to enjoy a cup of joe made from your personal supply of perfect water, nestling into your down sleeping bag by the fire you built.

Both destinations require work. You climb your way out of being stuck. You pace yourself through a season.

But look. I get it. Season or stuck, we must work for it. And either way, we're out of water, right? Shit.

Oh, I know this one! Thanks, Dad, for all pouring all your boy scout training into us girls growing up. You can get to your destination three ways.

Check Your Reserves

A good backpacker never lets themselves get so low on liquid, but it does happen. When backpacking, iodine is (as stated) a wonderful, dissolvable pill that kills the bacteria in water enough to be drinkable. (There are instructions, so, you know, follow those. I'm not claiming responsibility here, do your own field research when actually backpacking.) Iodine isn't any good if you don't have water.

That's why, although a good backpacker also reduces the weight she carries by limiting the resources she brings, she always has a backup bottle.

Check your reserves. Where in your "backpack of life" do you have a resource you forgot about? Just a little extra to keep you going for a while?

Partner Up

A well-planned solo trip can be cleansing for the soul.

Yet hiking in groups is highly recommended for safety reasons. Running out of water can be as dangerous as a bear encounter, and that's what friends are for. *En route* forward to the lake or up the mountain, having a buddy with you means you can do a little give-and-take to help each other get there. Maybe they've got plenty of water but could do with one of your extra protein bars. Sometimes our linear interactions (being supported by people who are right where we are, going through the same things as us) require a creative swap of resources.

For argument's sake, let's say you didn't start with a group. Even if you began this journey alone, you can find people along the way to help. There are some people out there, but just like the wide-open spaces of the Montana mountains in which I used to lose myself, sometimes you don't see another person for days. What are you supposed to do in the meantime, *die*?

Of course not, silly. You start your journey. The right person will be there to help; maybe they're just a little ahead of you. You need to close the gap and approach them with kind intentions if you want to reap the benefit of their resources.

Wait in the Rain

As with hiking in the Montana wilderness, this one is rarely the solution. But sometimes, we find ourselves utterly incapacitated. We don't see anyone around us who can spare a little water and moving isn't an option. If we stay here long enough, mother nature catches up with us and the clouds open into rain. You know how it goes, "when it rains, it pours."

Now you're motionless, wet, cold, alone, and you're *still* thirsty. You collapse on the nearest rock, or if you have any sense at all, you at least try to find shelter. Either way, you cower down and cry out desperately for an answer to your problem to just "show up."

How often do we lay down in our *rainy* valley, crying out for water to quench our thirst?

Sometimes the solution is pelting us, disguised as a storm, when all we have to do it stop using our hands to cover our teary eyes and reach them out, cupping them up toward the heavens?

Even if you've looked at your reserves, even if you don't have people along the journey to swap resources with, you can always receive extra provision in the storm if you look skyward.

(Dang son, someone shout amen for that.)

It's okay to be in a season, and it's okay to be on the climb. You can steady yourself through each, but don't mix up your paths. Don't start climbing when you should be marching.

A season, our marching period, is a time in life that can seem monotonous, joyless, or like it no longer contributes to the best of *you*. It can look like the answer is up, but it isn't. Yeah, I'm talking to all those new moms out there who've changed 300 diapers this week and are running on two hours of uninterrupted sleep per night. You can't give up your marching orders here and think the answer is at the top of the mountain. Walk through the tough times!

Not that the climb is any easier. You'll deal with the same feelings of monotony, joylessness, and lack of contributions to the best of you. Yup! I'm looking straight at you, twenty-two-year-old who complains about how your internship at the radio station hasn't "gotten you any closer to your dreams." And don't think for a hot second that I've forgotten about you, writer / poet / artist / sculptor / photographer / comedian / bullfrog (I don't know your life) who is still learning your craft and wants to give up.

The answer isn't walking away, it's climbing.

We all have "shitty" situations that don't match what we envisioned for our lives. It's okay to have seasons, it's okay to climb, and it's easy(ish) to tell the difference. Have a sit-down with yourself. Or, if inclined, have a meeting with your greater self (the Divine in you) to decipher which you're dealing with. We talk to ourselves because sometimes we need expert advice, you know. Or just go directly to the Big Cheese and talk out your shit.

Will this period pass in due time? Will it fulfill me once it has become a memory? Who are some of the people I admire and wish to emulate, and what seasons did they walk through? Can I find support with others going through the same season? Can I find support from those who have gone through a similar season? When I get out of this season, am I going to be able to help others?

And if you're still not sure, stick with the basics: Is my way out of this time of my life a march *through* it, or is it a climb *out* of it?

Shake Off Your Shit

Have you heard the story of the donkey with the broken leg? There once was a farmer, who, believing his donkey was as good as dead, dug a hole and tossed the donkey inside. I guess the vet wasn't an option for this asshole farmer, and he must have been out of bullets that day or something. Anyhow, the poor donkey (who just didn't deserve this shit), can't get out of the hole. Its leg is broken, remember?

Looking up to watch the sky for the last time, the donkey watched the farmer shovel dirt on its back. One spade at a time, the farmer covered the donkey's back.

However, the donkey knew this wasn't his season of death. So, he shook the dirt off, and stepped up. Every time the farmer tossed a shovelful in the hole, the donkey shook it off and rose. Until finally, the donkey had shaken off enough of the farmer's shit that it hobbled right out of that hole.

Whether you're walking through a season or overcoming a debilitating experience, keep shaking off the shit and stepping up.

Learn How to Ride Your Fucking Bike

You can ride a bike, right? Okay, even if you haven't done it in a while, you're familiar with how it works. Feet on pedals, hands on the handlebars, ass in the saddle, balance and go. Easy.

Have you ever seen someone ride a bike with one foot on the ground? I know, right? Can you imagine the road rash? It's a funny image, but what that really means is you can't. For a bike to actually ride, both feet need to be on the pedals and you need momentum to get started. The moment right before you get the momentum, however, can go either way. There're a few seconds of terror—I mean lag—when we lift our feet from the floor, push a little, and find our balance.

If done in the right order, the launch series works as intended. When done out of order, not so much. If you lifted your foot off the ground and tried to find your balance first, you'd probably fall. But by adding a touch of movement, we settle into our balance and find the momentum that keeps us propelled forward.

Stop using the excuse that you don't have balance in your life to mask the fact that you just won't take your foot off the ground. If you want to do this dumb sitting-in-the-saddle-shuffling-forward-on-one-foot-scoot-about thing, then it's going to take a long time to get to your destination. You could do it that way—the hard way—or you can just pick up your feet and ride your fucking bike.

Pick up your feet, *move,* and then find balance. It's the only way to go, trust me. You'll soon feel the breeze on your cheeks.

Channel Your Inner Creator

Visualization can be the best tool in your box when it comes to getting unstuck.

If you've never had an experience before, how can you know what it's like, right? And the unknown is scary. That which we do not know is so terrifying that we avoid it at all costs. We'll go as far as intentionally remaining in a habit or situation that we know isn't good for us because the alternative—the unknown—has us peeing in our pants.

Our brains are designed to keep us safe, remember? It's a giant, intricate filing system of the past, and when we're presented with new information, our brains pull out any file that is relatable. Our brains, scientifically, are designed to reflect everything we know in life, and this keeps it on a loop of experiences. Our brains are the intellectual and emotional records of all we've experienced.[3]

This leads us to do the same things we've always done, think what we've always thought, and remain stuck in a loop. We constantly put ourselves in situations that reaffirm our reality, because hey! It's all we know. Chemically, our brains ground us into our pasts.[4]

We are a predictable self. We loop through the same emotions because we always have, and we create a series of similar situations in our lives which will produce similar outcomes (to varying degrees), which cause us to continue to be that predictable self.

The good news is that once we start doing uncomfortable things and leaning into the unknown, our brain makes new connections. And every time we go through something we never thought we could go through and come out the other side wiser for it, we prove to our brains that making new connections is easy.[5]

If we're stuck, our brains keep us stuck. If we're moving, our brains keep us moving. So, we only need to get it from "stuck" to "moving," right?

How the *hell* do you do that?

You trick yourself into thinking you've already done the thing. You create a vision of the future instead of a memory of the past.

Even though our brains love their cozy little nests in the past, we're progressive creatures, always looking to grow. At a young age, we get these visions of what would make our lives "ideal." We dream big and have all the childish confidence in the world, believing we can have that life. We want to be astronauts and ballerinas. Then our grades go down, and we convince ourselves we don't belong amongst the stars. When our chubby little toes rip holes in our tights and our legs don't seem as graceful as Tina doing arabesques near the barre, we let that damn dream die. Circumstances challenge us, and we believe we aren't worthy of living our ideal life. And so, we settle.

Knowledge is the precursor to our future. The more knowledge we have, the more prepared we are for a new event in life. But get this: the neurological building process begins at contemplation. Boiled down, this means we create our own realities by imagining them.[6] Trippy, right?

When the speculative part of the brain turns on—the frontal lobe from which creativity blossoms—it starts sending messages to the rest of our brain that this possibility is okay. The frontal lobe is kind of like an expert recruiter, searching through your enormous filing system for the best solution, the best "woman for the job." It searches through all you've learned and experienced and comes up with a next step.[7]

We don't even need to go through an experience to know how we would handle it. We can come up with answers to everything, can't we? The people who give the "best" parenting advice don't even have kids. Heck, you'd probably do a better job as a politician than those clowns in office, huh? Just because we can come up with a solution doesn't mean we can make it a reality. The only thing that can do that is intention.

Let's do an exercise:

Think of a childhood dream you lost along the way. If you're hard up for one of the extreme ones like becoming a renowned mortician (don't laugh, that dream lasted at least a few years of my life), then drum up a dream that isn't too far gone; one from a year or two ago.

Got it?

Now take a minute to close your eyes. Picture yourself doing the thing. Maybe you're a model on the runway or a filmmaker. What is stopping you in this real world? Education, skills, looks? What if those things weren't holding you back in the version in your mind? In your mind, you can be anything, so really dig in. Envision that you're performing this passion and feel how fulfilling it is. Come on! Picture it; it's only an exercise, not a vow of commitment. Imagine you're amazing at what you do, and that all the obstacles you had to overcome to get to this point only added to your success. Your obstacles have become a secret sauce, the hurdles that gave you an edge. Now, visualize a young version of yourself approaching while you're fulfilling this dream, and young-you is amazed. What you were able to accomplish far surpassed what she could've dreamed.

Dumbfounded at your success, young-you asks how you did it. Older-you leans in to whisper, "You know all the stuff you think is going to be too hard to get through? Lean into that stuff. The hard stuff is what sets you apart and gets you ahead."

Young-you wants to smile, but all young-you musters is, "What!? I have to do hard stuff?"

Older-you affirms with a knowing smile. "Can I tell you another secret?"

Young-you quickly nods.

"None of that stuff is very hard, after all."

How does it feel to think that the thing that held you back all these years could've been what made you great? How does that cast-aside dream feel? Is there a sliver of sunlight?

Now that your mind believes that dream could come true again, find a possible step to take to propel that dream into action. I'm not going to ask you to commit, but be creative and think of one step you could take toward that dream right now.

I bet you thought of at least one thing.

Okay. So, one brief visualization exercise won't make all your dreams come true, but you know what it did? It helped you make a little movement, even if you don't yet know where the balance will come from.

You could start a new class, continue your education, or maybe it helped a name pop in your mind, someone who has been successful at that dream you once had who you can take out to coffee and learn from. You don't have to start pursuing that childhood dream again, though you can probably see at least one step to take.

Think about what would happen if you visualize your ideal life every day until something sticks? You can map out the start of this journey from nothing more than a vision. When you begin to mentally rehearse what that future day will be like, your brain begins to rewire with a chemical change.[8] And the more you rehearse, the more that ideal becomes reality.

The hardest part about change is not making the same choices you did the day before. Yup, I just basically said that the hardest part about change is change. (It's okay if you roll your eyes, I get it.) Change is damn hard. There *is* something that makes it easier.

Have you ever had lunch and then gone about the rest of your day not understanding why people keep giving you a weird look? And it isn't until your husband gets home with a, "Hey babe, you've got lettuce in your teeth" that you realize why the afternoon was so weird. Amplify that feeling by one hundred and then let it settle. Now ask yourself, is there a place in my life I've been stuck that I haven't noticed? Do I have "lettuce in my teeth?"

The first step toward making change easier is recognizing it.

The second is flossi—I mean, gentle self-correction.

We can recognize the faults of others because we look at them from a distance. Sometimes we don't look closely enough at ourselves to see the lettuce in our own teeth. When we recognize our faults from a distance— looking at them as if they belong to someone else—we can better see the extent of why and how they hinder us. We are more likely to let go of being "stuck" and let ourselves fall into the unknown abyss. At least there, we aren't writhing in stupidity (or lettuce teeth). Why from a distance? Because when we look at our old-self objectively and emotionally detached, we see things from a new angle and become aware of the root issues.

Start with an unbiased observation of your past self, and then renew your practice of visualizing the future again. Yeah, I sound like a 90s motivational speaker when I tell you to "visualize and attack," but it works. We can mentally rehearse again and again and reorganize the mind to create the future we want instead of reliving the past.

We already do this for our pasts, so why not do it for our futures? I mean, we've all had that one situation where someone wronged us, and it was unprovoked. I once stood through a twenty-minute line at the post office only to end up with my two-year-old son having a screaming fit while I paid for the box I was shipping. And on my exit, a rude old man clapped. He was so thrilled that I and my crying son were no longer in the building that he burst into applause. It stung, but I was so flabbergasted and put-off by the reality of the situation that I didn't respond. I just walked out of the building and cried in my car.

For the next few days, I rehearsed how that situation could've gone. I pictured myself yelling back at the man, or perhaps replying with a reciprocated round of applause and sarcastic comment about how my son, at *two-damn-years-old,* was more emotionally mature than this old fart. I even ran a scenario through my mind of what I thought the "perfect Christian" would say. In the end, I couldn't change the past. And when I thought through a multitude of scenarios, I couldn't honestly say I would've done anything differently.

This is why we place an intention and then self-correct. Whether you know it or not, you could be moments away from a situation like that. Or, you could be right around the corner from your destiny. It's all about how you choose to respond. And if you're a good little Boy Scout and you're always prepared, you will have made that choice in advance by being intentional.

This doesn't involve chronic overthinking. No, your brain is used to doing that, and without success. By being intentional, mindful, and by gently self-correcting, we can create a better future and unstick ourselves from our stuck places.

Also—and this last step may sound like it's just for fun but don't buy it, it's work, too, so take it seriously—we need to celebrate our damn selves. Part of self-correcting is recognizing the good choices we make. When we're grateful for something, we put an "emotional signature" on it and claim it as our own. This actually makes it happen to us more because our brains have now made a new connection, and moving forward, our brain will help us get to that rewarding connection over and over.[9]

So, when you're reflecting on your day, don't just think about all the things you could do better next time, also concentrate on how you can pat your damn back. When you make better behavior choices and have more self-advancing thoughts and habits, celebrate it! This is how we make those rewired places become permanent hardware.

ANXIOUS
Freaking the Fuck Out

Before settling into the glory of the Inland Northwest, my family spent one magical year in Austin, Texas. What a great city, y'all. Even when the scorpions stung and the seasons refused to change, we loved our time in Bat City. From the scent of BBQ wafting through the vibrant streets to the wax museum of horror film characters, we let the weirdness smother us in a warm, thrilling blanket.

With our girls old enough that I could be away without too much guilt, I hungered to try something new. I found a part-time job working the front desk of a wedding chapel in the south hills. It wasn't challenging, but the work culture was a dream. My job was easy: run the front, restock the cooler, and issue refunds for all the deposits these shiny couples put down for their big day. That's right; after the main event you got your money back, this little chapel has always been free to use.

Y'all. This is no regular wedding chapel. Chapel Dulcinea was the passion project of Roy Williams, best-selling author of *The Wizard of Ads* trilogy, and his lovely wife, Pennie. As a renowned author and teacher, marketing wiz, and owner of The Wizard Academy and Wizard Academy Press, Roy flooded his giant property with anything Don Quixotesque. To say he was merely a fan would be blasphemous. From the architecture and Spanish décor to the names of the buildings, from the bronze statues to the giant wind chimes, this placed dripped the Quixotic ideal that anything could happen. So, with the love interest to whom the great Don always devoted his acts of heroism, the free chapel was christened Dulcinea and adorned with romantic idealism. Plus, the place was cute as shit. Look it up.

The Williams were fascinating people to work for, and though my time with them was brief, I took many of their teachings that continue serving me. But most lessons came from the "men on the ground." Although the great Roy Williams could look down from the stucco tower of his cleverly created domain, the spirit of Chapel Dulcinea remains with those whose participated in the chapel's ceremonies. The stories of those who spoke sacred words under the chapel roof are the true vestibules for the Quixotic notion that an ideal, romantic utopia can exist.

The fun thing about working with weddings is the front row seat the job provides to the vast array of ways people deal with situations. We're all at least mildly familiar with how weddings work. No matter the traditions or religions which are incorporated, the formula is the same. Loved ones meet to honor the joining of two people in marriage, some nice things are said, some pictures are taken, and guests usually celebrate with some food and maybe a dance or two. Although the ceremonies can vary, the sizes can differ, and the budgets can fluctuate, weddings happen with the same general rhythm, and they all pivot on two little words. "I do."

That's what made working for a free chapel so cool; some people would use the site for the intended purpose of vow proclamation before caravanning to a reception elsewhere. Others stayed to use the paid reception facilities, spending loads on the romantic site. I saw the glitz and glam that a 60k budget could get, and I watched young couples sprint through the rain at the least desirable time slot of 8 am, wearing vintage rentals. I witnessed very anxious brides and grooms lash out at their friends and family when cakes were late, or guests were rowdy. And I watched the sincerest demonstrations of affection between people who had nearly nothing but each other.

One bride in particular stunned us all in a flowing silk gown that hugged her perfectly curved back. Her hair twisted effortlessly at the nape of her bronzed neck, adding a sunset glow of vibrancy to the red rose tucked in her ear. The mariachi band played in the distance as both laughter and tequila were passed around in the warm dusk of the Texas summer.

In the bustle of the pre-ceremony celebration, while guests loosened up with libations for what was sure to be the dreamiest sunset wedding of the season, that lovely bride disappeared. With everyone assembled under the wooden beams of the open-air chapel on the cliff, waiting for the ceremony to begin, the father of the bride burst into the front building where my desk resided, worried sick because no one could find his *Princesa*. We dispersed the troops, sending the staff to the dressing rooms, the honeymoon suite, and even the reception area to assure she wasn't making last minute adjustments to the table settings or something. When her husband caught wind of her disappearance, he used his eager husbandly intuition and checked the parking lot, and we all followed like the worried search party we were.

Her car was gone.

The man whipped out his phone and got her on the line. Although I couldn't understand what he was saying, his frantic tone spoke of "Where the hell are you?" When she was no longer on the other end, he yelled her name into the dead receiver; his eyes widened and fixed onto the horizon beyond the line of rosemary bushes.

Voices mumbled in the distance as we—parents of the bride, the husband, the planner, the photographer, and the Chapel Dulcinea crew— stood there aghast that the seemingly perfect bride would skip out on her own wedding. With our eyes glued to the empty gravel parking spot, a soft whimper came from the would-be husband. Then, because it must've hit him like a tidal wave, this six-foot, Benjamin Bratt look-alike crumpled to the gravel. He cried out in a pain that didn't require me to understand Spanish to discern.

Time fell away as we all settled into the realization of what was going on.

Until we heard the crunch of tires on gravel and saw headlights turn into the lot. The bride, in her glowing perfection, leaped from the vehicle and crashed into the arms of her husband to-be. What happened next was a rapid string of passionate kissing, intermingled with words I later had interpreted to me by a bilingual crew member.

As it turned out, the bride, in her mad rush to get to the venue on time, forgot to turn off her curling iron at his home—the house they were going to live in together from this day forward—where her friend did her hair. Plagued with worry that the happiest day of her life could become the worst if she burned down her new husband's home, she found a window of opportunity to leave and check on the house. Except the drive took longer than she planned, and as the cell reception in the hills cut in and out, her husband was unable to hear her on the call.

Because she was so afraid of perceived danger, this bride unknowingly let her husband believe the worst. And although it worked out in the end, their varied perceptions remained strikingly different. She had a fear that cycled through her mind with enough intensity and insistence that she dropped everything to attend to it. He, on the other hand, probably wouldn't have cared if she'd burned down their house. I mean, the way that man kissed that woman in the parking lot as though he'd never hold her again convinced me he couldn't have cared less about the house.

They overcame a perceived loss, and that sweetness added to their vows. Every cheek was tear-soaked by the end of the ceremony, and they all celebrated into the night.

The best part?

She hadn't left the curling iron on, after all.

As the reception kicked into full swing, the bride admitted this to the wedding planner, who later told us that when she arrived to check on the device, it was unplugged and put away; she just didn't remember doing it. They (thankfully) had a good laugh about it.

The curling iron *could* have burned the house down, sure. It's entirely possible that, via fluke accident, it could have spontaneously combusted near a can of hairspray and blown up the house. Why not? Anything's possible. But it wasn't very likely, was it? Even if the iron had been left on, the likelihood that it would become hot enough to burst into flames or blow the outlet are slim. The worst-case scenario wasn't the most-likely scenario, yet she let it control her thoughts and subsequently modify her behavior.

I wonder which is worse: worrying about something that isn't the most-likely scenario or allowing the anxiety of the situation to dictate our actions.

How many times have we missed opportunities because we were busy chasing down a "dangerous curling iron?" What have you overlooked in life because you've been focused on worry and not the beauty around you?

Although real anxiety disorders can cause debilitation from change and an inability to redirect one's thinking or focus, we all too often become bound by worry as if it were a disorder too.

Worry happens as a result of focusing on events in the future that may never take place. Intrusive thoughts associated with anxiety can become debilitating, leading to fear and negativity about what's to come. Anticipating these perceived disastrous events not only squashes potential opportunities but can also lead to self-fulfilled prophecies, or pain felt twice. And what if the event never happens? Then we have suffered for nothing.

Repeat after me: worry is bad.

You can change these patterns of thinking. We can anticipate a multitude of options following any situation without having only the negative potential outcomes rule us.

In other words, stop practicing everything to death. Stop rehearsing the worst possible scenarios in your mind so much that you make it more likely to happen. We don't get what we want; we get what we focus on. The more you go over the outcome you anticipate in your mind, the more you "manifest" that outcome. Did the bride manifest a fire in the home because of the curling iron that wasn't even plugged in? No, but she focused on her worry so much that she nearly caused a "fire" in their wedding by not showing up.

With practice and a few tips, you can let go of your anxiety and trust yourself to be able to handle whatever outcome occurs. Over time, you will earn your own trust, and the outcomes of any situation won't matter; you'll know you can handle it.

Life is anxiety producing. (Duh, right?) From the ladder climbing we do at work to attending to the notifications on our phones, we live on the edge of our seats that something may go horribly wrong. Especially as women, we tend to keep a lot of plates turning and operate under the false impression that if we let go of our focus on each plate for a second, it's all going to crash down upon us.

The expansive history of human development has wired us to be on high alert for survival, so we spend our lives on the cusp of breakdowns far more often than necessary. We become anxious about everything and then get anxious about our anxiety until all the walls cave around us. Fucking awful, right? We forget what it's like to be truly at peace.

With our energy draining into the worry, we have little left for creativity, love, fulfillment, or beauty. Which is what makes our bride's story so ironic: the idealism of the Quixotic mind stands for the notion that anything can happen. Yet her anxiety and worry produced just one possibility—the worst outcome.

Anxiety causes our dreams to bleed out, and without our idealism, we live with lack. We can't be both Quixotic and anxious. So, let's don our bucket helmets like the great Don and do some anxiety triage.

Anchor Your Damn Breath

If you're cynically inclined, I urge you to resist rolling your eyes at that one. Yeah, it sounds a little bogus, but what do we tell the woman pushing out a baby? Breathe! When someone's in pain—the birthing variety or any other—we're conditioned to advise the concentration on this simple process. Coaches, elite runners, and pro ballers all advocate for the importance of breathing right during peak performance.

But when it comes to our nerves, we misassociate this anchoring technique as a nearly-comical act. We roll our eyes and scoff when someone recommends we "just breathe." Anchoring yourself into your breath is way more than a sitcom-worthy gimmick of breathing into a brown paper bag (that is no longer recommended by professionals, by the way).

We only have one life. We can't get back a breath we already breathed, nor can we breathe a breath for the future. We get this moment we're in, and the next, if we're lucky. What might happen if you lived fully in this breath, and then fully in the next?

If breath anchoring sounds boring to you, let's spice it up and call it "fuuuuucking breath anchoring," because you can add a curse word to this practice if you want to. Spice it up.

Let's practice now so you can memorize this tactic when worry strikes and panic looms. Take a moment to get comfortable and then close your eyes. Take a slow breath in, feeling the air fill your lungs and make your belly rise. Then, encourage your exhale to be one second longer than the inhale and repeat this several times. By concentrating on the length of the exhale, we can trick our bodies into calming down, anchoring us in the moment. And, like I said, if you need to let out a slow "fuuuuuuuuck" on the exhale, do it.

Keep breathing and feeling what it's like to be present in this moment. Then, take a moment to go inward. Look at the problem from different angles. Think of at least three solutions. When you picture each, it's okay to feel anxiety in the moment. You're safe now; you're only imagining the outcome, after all. Let the anxious feels come and go as you tally each possible outcome until the right solution presents itself.

Is the curling iron going to catch the curtains on fire? No, they're five feet away.

Will it combust and blow a hole in the sink? Probably not.

Even if the worst happens, will I physically be okay? Yes, but I still want the nagging idea of danger to go away.

Can I call a neighbor to check for me instead of leaving my wedding? Sure, or perhaps I could send my crazy nephew who won't stop trying to flirt with the caterer anyway. He needs something productive to do.

Once you've rehearsed a few examples, act on your solution and take it one step at a time until the problem is solved. Then, once you've put out that mental fire, move to the next and the next, going down in order of importance. This type of triage may cause you to give up things or people in your life, and it may even make some people dislike you. You must decide what you will need to give up in order to be peaceful.

Sometimes you only need to let go of your own mental blocks, other times it means you may have to sever or distance yourself from relationships that perpetuate negative feelings. If you struggle to get your job done on time, then maybe you need to ask the person in the cubicle next to you to stop making small talk every time you're balls-deep on a project. Perhaps we'll have to let go of being "perfect" and allow ourselves to just be.

Let it the Fuck Go

I get it. We want to control outcomes because we think we know what's best for ourselves. We freak about whether we'll get into a specific school or get that job we worked hard for. We try to manage the results of every circumstance. Yet in doing so, we could miss our calling—the thing which leads us to our greatest fulfillment in life—because we're busy chasing something that wasn't meant to be.

Sometimes, what we think we want is holding us back from getting what we were meant to have.

One Sunday afternoon, a twelve-year-old son tagged along with his father. After completing his errand list at the mall, the father told the son it was time to go; they had one more thing to do before going home. The son thought he had been very patient by now while they visited the tailor and chose appropriate shoes for the father's upcoming work function. The son could've spent the afternoon playing video games or hanging out with a pizza and a movie, but instead, he patiently followed, figuring he owed his dad a solid.

On their way out, he noticed a row of mini helicopters lining a kiosk in the middle of the hall. As the clerk whizzed the demo copter in and out of the crowd, the son visualized playing with the toy in the backyard later that day with the sun on his face. Surely, this small device would bring the greatest joy; what better reward could he ask for after a laborious hour in the mall?

"Can I have one of those?" the son asked.

"No," said the father.

"Why not?" the son protested. Why couldn't his dad see the joy this would bring? Didn't he want his son to be happy? It wasn't asking too much.

"Trust me," said the father.

"But…"

"Every moment you spend arguing with me takes away from what is next, son."

"Nothing could be better," said the son. "I don't want whatever you have in store for me; I want one of those!"

The father gave only a silent glance at the helicopters.

"No."

Throwing his hands up, the son begrudgingly dragged himself behind his father. He grumbled the whole way to the car and all along the ride. His dreams of operating a remote-control helicopter were shattered, and he decided he was never going to let it go. If it took the rest of his life, the son was going to make his dad see how unfair this situation was.

A few minutes and multiple eye rolls later, they arrived at their final stop; a helicopter tour of the city. The son was never meant to fiddle this thumb on a cheap, plastic remote control. He was meant to fly in a real helicopter and see the world.

If you can't let go of what you think you need, you'll never be open to the possibility that there's a greater option out there. And maybe, just *maybe*, you'll put your foot down for the thing you know you want, and you'll get it. You'll fly your little remote-control helicopter and it might bring you joy. What have you missed out on?

Don't miss out on your destiny because you're too busy chasing your momentary desires.

Not to Do

By pulling our focus away from the worst-case scenario and releasing anxious feelings, we can quickly and painlessly find our way to peace. However, just "letting go" isn't so easy for some… nay, *most*. Have you ever pulled a rope so hard it left a burning imprint in your hand? To avoid that, many will never release the rope. If you're the type of person whose anxiety is wrapped up in the tight grip of your accomplishments, then holy hell do I have a solution for you.

Throw away your "to do" list. Chuck it. Burnt it. Turn it into a paper airplane and release it off a cliff.

Okay, when you're done gasping and waving your hand like an offended Southern belle, let me give you some good news. You don't need that thing. I know, I know. I thought the same thing. "How will I remember what the kids need to be doing? What will happen to my schedule? What if I miss something important? What if I *die*?"

You won't die. You'll probably miss something (let's face it, you probably would have forgotten something, anyhow). And your schedule will be fine.

If you're like me and live by lists, just the suggestion of ditching it causes anxiety. I imagine it's much like what the hostess of a busy Manhattan restaurant whose night is booked with back-to-back reservations would feel if the guest book vanished. There would be mayhem and panic. How in God's name could anyone come back from that level of tragedy?

Slow down, you. Breathe in, exhale "fuuuuuck." Think anchoring thoughts.

Let me ask you something. If your list gives you anxiety, how is it serving you? You might feel like you'll fall apart without it, but if it hasn't been holding your life together either, then maybe it isn't vital. Maybe we don't have to be addicted to the sound our pencil makes when it crosses an item off and instead can look for the joy that's passing by while our noses are stuck in a book of lists.

This doesn't just go for day-to-day to-do lists we make on paper. What about the lists we make for ourselves in our life? Live an abundant single life where I travel the world. Check. Get married. Check. Have babies and teach them how amazing travel is. Check!

Things don't always go the way we think they will, do they? We fight and claw our way to the exact life we thought we wanted, but it's full of exhaustion and unmet expectations. What if we weren't meant to be child-carrying globetrotters? Instead, we were meant to teach social studies to inner-city kids.

It's okay if we have a task list, we just don't need to be glued to it. I'm not saying we shouldn't be organized, prepared, and properly scheduled; those are all great tools for streamlining life and achieving things. Maybe we should start each day with a fresh piece of paper and prioritize what's important first. What if we didn't write down any task until we had fresh eyes on our priorities.

Don't make me tell you about the time I had a tooth ache that was so bad, I drug my body through hell for five days until I had an opening in my schedule. Might I remind you, I'm the *boss* of my company? As big cheese, I should've been able to tell everyone, "I'm out" and get my cavity filled. Don't make me draw another analogy between a dental emergency and that anxiety-producing mental cavity you keep ignoring.

When we become anxious, we go into "reactive mode," and good things rarely come from being reactive. Instead, be proactive by anticipating the result you want, not looking for a way the scenario might not work. Focus on what you want and follow the steps needed to get there. Take it moment by moment, and before you know it, you've bypassed the anxiety by having created a better life.

If we don't let go of our to-do lists, we run the risk of managing today based on yesterday's priorities, and we close ourselves off from the opportunities that lie *beyond* our own agendas. Yes, we can craft some pretty cool projects in our life. I'm all for planning and striving. But we have to be open to the possibility that our answer isn't written on our little pieces of paper.

Despite our best efforts, we aren't always capable of predicting the correct path between point A and point B. Yes, you can map out your journey and what you want it to look like, and you can assemble the best way you believe will make this dream happen. You should also be open to the possibility that the best option for you is one you never thought of.

The best options, after all, usually come into our lives disguised as problems and challenges and U-turns.

Trust yourself to know what to do. No matter what happens in any situation, you can handle yourself. You are not bound to a single outcome.

Honor Your Rituals

Rituals are usually ignored and often undervalued. Without them, we lack the stability our minds need to handle things. We can better face the uncertainties of life when we are grounded in cast-iron rituals. Tasks we perform regularly become an emotional home base upon which we can return when feeling anxious.

Rituals help us honor the rhythm of life. When we feel flooded with worry, we can return to our rituals as proof that there is a time for everything.

I'm not encouraging you to light a bunch of candles, stand on your head, and twirl around three times. That's dangerous. Don't do that. Rituals can literally be anything. The wide variety of cultural differences is global proof that our rituals can be anything. Some people light incense and pray, while others collect at the family table to enjoy a nightly meal without fail. You bet your ass dinner is a ritual. Even sleep is.

Just like the circadian rhythm of our bodies, we need cycles. For all the stormy stuff that happens outside, we need a calm place to land inside. Rituals help us sink into that calm place. Like the breathing exercise, rituals anchor us.

So, pick something you love and do it with daily (or near daily) consistency.

A few things to keep in mind while creating your ritual:

Make sure it's healthy. Flopping on the couch at the end of the day with a bucket of fried chicken might be an appealing ritual, but you need one that will serve you. Instead, indulge in your favorite show while doing some gentle stretching and enjoying an iced tea.

Return to it often. Even if I don't meditate every day, if I go a day or two without it, I can feel the anxiety bubble inside. My mind is like an over-hyper Weimaraner. In order to be calm, I need to first run my mind and let it release all the pent-up energy that's in there. With the focus and mindful mental exercise of meditation, I release all the yuck in my mind. Without doing it regularly, I could miss out on the compounding growth that occurs when we practice something daily.

Allow your rituals to change. You may find that a ritual that once served you no longer adds value to your day, and that's okay. We evolve and grow, and so should our rituals. We can feel crap out and allow ourselves grace to change things up. You may go a month getting up at 5am to fill your cup before your family wakes up, and then find the next month that doesn't serve you at all. Instead, a quiet moment during nap time for the kids is where you find your peace.

Borrow from the greats. Learn what people who have the kind of life you want to emulate do. If you're striving to own a successful business, then learn how successful entrepreneurs start their day. Think of someone you admire; what are their rituals?

Make them mindful so they contribute to your goals. If you want to strengthen your marriage, make a ritualistic time to be together every day after work for twenty straight minutes of catch up before you do anything else. If your dream is to run a marathon for your fortieth birthday, maybe every morning while eating your oatmeal and sipping that banana shake you make daily, you visualize yourself crossing the finish line. And when you sprain your ankle and can't run it until your forty-first, you stick out the ritual until it happens because you're not a damn quitter.

Choose your rituals carefully so you can trust them to be your "safe place" to land. When we nurture a safe place in one area, we can grow in another.

Be Quixotic

The idea of Quixotism isn't just defined by being idealistic, romantic, or utopic. The term Quixotic is also defined as ideas that are impractical, frivolous, or futile. It's in this vision that the "Don Quixotes" of the world wander around wearing a bucket for a helmet and dedicating battles to a lovely lady named "Dulcinea" who he's *never even met*. It is foolish; a vain attempt to live out a fantasy that will never happen. Quixotic people—us romantics that believe in utopia despite how futile the attempt—can be seen as ridiculous.

So-fucking-what?

We chase dreams that may never happen, so-fucking-what? There's joy in the journey.

We pine for dreams-come-true when the world is against us, so-fucking-what? The dream is half the fun.

Your helmet is a bucket, so-fucking-what? You're protected.

Don't miss out on your opportunity to be your own "Don Quixote" because you're anxious about all the things you're not.

A Quixotic person is someone who believes she can solve world hunger, even if she is "just" one person with one idea.

A Quixotic person refuses to accept that his business is failing. He continues to find a way to pull through and take the steps to turn things around, even when the likelihood of his success is dismal.

A Quixotic person doesn't let the outside voice of improbability overtake their dream.

Perhaps the greatest way to release the anxiety of the future is by marrying ourselves with the idea that we can have what we dream, despite the odds. My journey will take battles and people will laugh at my bucket, but if I proclaim my utopia is achievable, then I have nothing to worry about. Eventually, I will get there, and it will be worth it.

One breath at a time, you can let your anxiety pass. One "idealistic" thought at a time, you can train your brain to look at the best possible outcome for any situation. And since we get what we focus on, if we focus on getting the best outcome instead of being anxious about the worst, we might actually beat the odds and make our own utopia.

LONELY Damned Loser

My father is a retired minister. Because of his position, for the past 30-plus years, I've been given more than just the title of "preacher's kid" and the pigeonholed perception that I must have been rebellious. I was given a front row seat to human behavior. The gift of witnessing so many life-changing moments has made every stereotype about *my kind* worth it. Many of my truest friends have come out of my church upbringing, and the lessons have saved my life numerous times over. I've seen people come out of emotional bondage and overcome addictions. I've seen families restored and marriages put back together because of the counseling of the beautiful man I have the privilege to call Dad.

When I was a kid, we lived in a medium-sized town in the dead center of Montana.

I remember one Saturday when my dad went to perform a funeral for a homeless man. In situations where a member of the community passed who had no resources, family, or care to handle the expenses, the city called my dad. My father was a part of a small number of pastors who volunteered their time and energy to perform the ceremonies that nobody else wanted to perform. These beautiful leaders understood that they could contribute to the last memories of people and pay respects with their small sacrifice of time.

As far as I remember, this particular homeless man had a few people that the city attempted to reach out to. Whether they were friends or family, I'm not sure. I do remember my dad telling my mom in the kitchen as he straightened his collar and refilled his coffee that he was expecting a small graveside attendance.

He showed up, and there wasn't anyone there. It was just my dad, the man in the casket, and the fucking rain.

To my dad, this was unacceptable.

Putting the ceremony on hold—because who was going to complain?—my dad came home and knocked on the door of the man who lived beside us, who played the bagpipes. In a few words, Dad coerced the man out of his easy chair and told him to grab his instrument. Then, my dad came home, made a bunch of phone calls, and headed back into the rain.

The cemetery was city owned and conveniently near the downtown area, so Dad took to the streets. He went out of his comfort zone and stopped people who were just trying to go about their day and begged them to honor this life.

"Even if you don't remember how he smiled and waved at people outside of the library, this person mattered!" he said, speaking to the core of humanity. *This person mattered.*

With a small company now in tow, he returned to the side of the grave and performed the ceremony. As the crowd trickled in, a small buzz spread, and a few more strangers gathered to become momentary friends. With his passionate words, all attendees were in tears as they fought for a view of the man in the casket who was now being seen off properly. Because my dad believed this one soul counted, everyone in attendance assumed it was true.

Because it was. My dad has the innate ability to peer into the souls of people and see their purpose. He can pull it out, help you nurture that seed, and then smile gently as it grows into a beautiful bouquet of spiritual flowers. He's the kind old witch in every fantasy movie who touches the barren ground with her staff and magically makes a garden grow.

This is how I remember my father being a minister.

But as much as I don't want to dwell on them, I can also recall the shitty moments.

I remember when my dad did the funeral for someone who personally and deeply mattered to him, only to have attendees smash beers and do donuts in the parking lot, never offering him even a kind word of thanks or consoling him for *his* loss, too.

I remember when he put everything into new appointments, with the energy of a young man hoping to grow a church that was dying, only to watch the congregation dismiss him for not wanting to be their puppet.

I remember when he got a series of angry letters about how he preached "too much Bible." He didn't sound like the motivational preachers on TV, and so his messages got tuned out, even though incorporating scripture was literally his job description. I remember the sorrow, the heartache, the disappointment of pouring into people who never gave back.

Now in his retirement, he should be surrounded by many who love him unconditionally and thank him for the service he gave to God and his communities, as he just tried to make the world a little better. But instead, I watch him tinkering with his cars (away from people) and backpacking (to *really* get away from people), not wanting to open himself up anymore and be vulnerable because too many of the wounds are still fresh. Deep emotional wounds don't heal overnight, and I know he's going through a season of restoration. And I'm proud of him for taking time to do the things he loves now after 30 years of service.

You know what really sucks? Now that he's retired, he should be flooded with invitations. He should be taken out to coffee on occasion, be invited to dinner parties, asked to join softball leagues—why not? He's in good shape. He should at least be invited to hunt on more friends' properties or get a dang thank you card from someone he served over the last three decades.

He doesn't say this out loud, but I worry that my dad is lonely. It's a feeling I'm all-too-familiar with, so maybe I'm just projecting my loneliness onto him (forgive me if I am). And if he is, he has every right to be. After all, he gave of himself for too long without emotional compensation.

If you're lonely, I would hazard a bet that you became this way at some point in your journey because your energy was draining out into someone who never gave it back. And because of that, you decided that you only deserved to be in relationships where you gave, and they took.

Tragically, most of our loneliness isn't born from isolation. It comes after giving energy to people who never returned it with the same volume and enthusiasm as it was given. When we give to others and they don't reciprocate, we convince ourselves we are those other curse words— worthless, disappointed, fragile—and we end up lonely. We train ourselves to believe that we only deserve the relationships we must exhaust ourselves to be in; we no longer want to take part in relationships. *Then,* we isolate.

Fortunately, there's a great cure for loneliness. There are approximately 7.4 billion of them, actually. In the same way food fills our bellies, people fill our souls. In different portions and varieties, we can surround ourselves with amazingness… and I'm not just talking about my favorite curry buffet.

Before addressing how to gather the right people into your life (so we ensure we're getting the right flavors, quantities, and nutritional variety… okay, I might still be talking about food), let's make room for them by doing a little relational excavation.

Bye, Felicia—Give Energy Where Energy is Returned

I wonder if you have any relationship energy-drains?

Me: Got any relationship energy-drains?
You: Myra, I don't know what the hell you're talking about.
Me: Check it. I've got examples.

An energy-drain is the new coworker who saunters in and bogarts all your watercooler buddies, making you feel isolated. Maybe you have a friend who monopolizes your time whenever you're together, always interrupting your story, problem, or joy with the phrase, "Well, you know what happened to me?" Or, you volunteer your time at the charity you're passionate about but are never treated as if they need you or appreciate that you're there.

It's okay to pour into others; the Bible asks us to do it. Any religion with human goodness at the heart supports the claim that we spend a portion of our lives in self-sacrifice to others. We often stop there and forget that the energy needs to flow back to us for this act of giving to be fulfilling—to us, to the recipient, and to God. We were created to perpetuate the beauty of the world with our acts, yet how are we supposed to do that if we only give time to people who drain us?

It starts with misunderstanding what to look for in reciprocated energy. Let's say you spend a week in Honduras building houses; your materialistic mind is going to come at you with, *Don't do this; you won't get anything out of it.* But the energy you get back from the act of service comes in heart-changing moments, a different perspective on your world at home, and the satisfaction of seeing all the happy tears. In return for the energy my dad poured into the stranger's funeral, he got to watch people wake up from their mundane existence, and for a moment, they were all given the gift of understanding how fleeting life can be. Everyone in attendance went home and looked at their life a little differently, and *that's* the ultimate form of reciprocated energy.

Even in the day-to-day, energy exchanges happen on a small scale. The drains tally until most of our "give a fuck" reserves have run out. This is when we often grab a match to burn us some bridges.

(And although I will never be the one to tell you not to burn a bridge—especially to those who caused you physical or mental harm—I think we do it a *smidge* too often. It's okay to let people walk in and out of your life when a natural distance has formed between you. But if you have more enemies than friends, you may be doing something wrong. A good look in the mirror might be in order. Just saying, sisters.)

You don't have to say goodbye to everyone in your life who is gobbling up your energy. I mean, none of us would have kids if we did that. Just pay attention. We are in charge of setting the stage for reciprocated energy.

Look, we don't knowingly and intentionally misappropriate our energy. I would never come out and say it's your fault you're lonely. But… it kind of is. You didn't do it on purpose. In fact, you got exactly what you wanted by pouring out to others and not expecting to get anything back.

We adopt this noble idea that the act of giving is fulfilling in itself, yet we teach our children to expect a return on energy with kind friendships, "pleases and thank yous," and other basic manners. If our kids should expect a return of energy (a "thank you" from someone after performing a kindness), why can't we?

This world requires a give-and-take. If all you do is give, give, *give,* and you never get back, then your spirit begins to see the dark side, leaving you open to a new list of curse words. Cynical. Ornery. Resentful. Yeah, guess who gets hurt by those curse words? You and everyone around you. So please, remind me why it's selfish to protect your spirit?

For instance, let's say you started a side hustle and feel called to kindly give away your talents. You figure a few pro-bono jobs will gain you a fan base, and then you can start charging for your services. Except, those few free jobs didn't promote you, leave a review, or say anything more than a quick "thanks." You start to believe you don't deserve to get paid for this, after all. When the truth is the person benefiting from your freebies didn't appreciate what you did for them because it required no investment on their end.

Now, it's okay to give your talents away if, in return, you reel in a fan base; people start asking to purchase whatever it is you're offering; you get energy back that sustains you for the next step. But if you fall into a cycle of always giving and never receiving, then you don't have the funds necessary (financial or emotional) to stay open.

Think of your life as a business.

- Where are you bleeding energy and not getting it in return?
- Which relationships are you in that suck the life out of you?
- Can you let those relationships or obligations go?
- What pieces of your past do you keep reliving in your mind that make you feel as though you're not worthy of having energy returned to you?
- How can you exchange your energy better so a return is guaranteed?

We are taught to serve and mimic God when we give without expectation because that's how God gives to us: without expectation. But what happens when you stop taking from God and start giving back by passing along the blessings He's given you?

If you want to experience everything God has for you, maybe you need to start giving God everything you've got.

(Okay, I promised not to be preachy, but damn. Someone needed that nugget right there.)

Mother Yourself

As the mother of small children, I know no one will care for them and look out for their well-being like me. Their grandparents love them, their teachers care, their doctors want them to be healthy, and they even have an awesome lineup of babysitters and friends of mine who support them. But no one will look out for their well-being like I will. No one.

Cemented to me from birth, these little babes could literally take a shit on my face while I slept, and I'd still wipe their tushies the next day. They could open the cage to a tiger at the zoo, and I'd still fight that tiger to the death for their safety. If you're a parent, you're familiar with this weird biological glitch… I mean principle.

Even if you have a strong tribe, you ultimately should give more shits about your kids than other people. It's why we get so heated when we debate vaccines, learning practices, and equal rights. We love these little fuckers so much that we put their pictures all over the place and dream of what they'll be when they grow up. It's why we cry out for their safety and well-being.

Why don't we do that for ourselves? Okay, I'm not saying hang pictures of yourself all over the place—even if a good selfie-sesh is good for the soul. I mean, why don't we fight for our welfare the way we fight for the well-being of our offspring?

If you're used to mothering anyone in any way (dogs and parakeets included, why not?) then let's scoot-scoot a little mirror before those lovely eyes of yours and let's use that mom-magic on yourself.

Give a shit about how you're treated by others, even if it must be through the lens of your "inner mother." Hike up your Lululemon workout pants and go to war for yourself.

And when it comes to mothering and protecting ourselves, there's a huge way we can do that that most people forget about. This one is super important, so I'll say it clearly so there's no confusion:

Stop letting others believe in your dreams more than you do.

Yes, it's a blessing when someone comes alongside us and believes in the thing we want for our lives. Yoking with someone who wants the best for you can contribute to a quicker and more fulfilling journey. But if they see it for you more than you do, you have some vision problems that need adjusting.

There are going to be times when we lose faith in ourselves and need others to bolster our dreams with a little heave-ho. But this shouldn't be the norm. If you're living your life with little belief left in yourself—and many lonely people are—then the solution is in you.

(Ladies and gentlemen, that right there is the key lyric of every diva song ever written.)

Yeah, the solution is in you.

So, get your "mom on" and scream like you're the one about to score the winning point for the soccer game. This time, cheer for yourself! You're a badass and you've got this.

Find Your Tribe

My daughter runs cross country, and her meets are the highlight of my week. She usually places in the top and has been known to smoke the boys. We're very proud of her, and we make it known: she's positive, dedicated, and a great teammate who supports her fellow runners.

We teach our kids that supporting others is important, so I stand right alongside her after each race and cheer on the other kids. You know, "model the behavior you want to teach." Pretty simple.

Because of this, I get to watch all the runners, and my favorite ones are the ones who come in last. Have you ever seen this? A kid lacks the ability to pace themselves properly and falls behind. That, or maybe the kid runs like I do—like a turkey caught in the mud. I know what it's like to force my exhausted body forward in an act that makes my limbs tighten, causes my lungs to scream, and forces my cheeks to look like I'm slowly morphing into a tomato. I admire these participants the most. Not only do they continue to show up and participate at something they continually place last in, but they finish their race.

Here's what I've learned from these fabulous kiddos:

- The ones who come in last push themselves hard to finish;
- They're surrounded by people cheering them on, and;
- They feel the victory just as much as the people who came in before them.

I see it in their little faces as they amble across the finish line with puffer-fish cheeks and a stitch in their side; they are happy to be done.

Just like everyone else, they get to say, "I did it."

For the most part, they're proud of themselves. Sure, they sometimes finish with long stretches between them and the person in front of them. Sometimes they're lapped completely. Sometimes they're discouraged. In the end, there are hugs from family or high-fives from coaches and teammates to make them feel better.

The resolve on their little faces is something I can get behind and emulate in my own life. Because how many of us fall behind on something, and instead of finishing, we just give up? And how many more are standing on the sideline because they didn't have the courage to try? I'm sorry, but if a kindergartner in a cast can finish his race, we can all finish ours.

It's been years since I could run an eight-minute mile. Were I to compete against a bunch of second graders, I would probably come in last.

Relating to these mini-racers goes deeper than my running pace. If lives have themes, finishing last might be mine. I never finish as fast as my competitors, but I'll be damned if I don't finish with everything I've got.

Instead of feeling bad that you're behind everyone and isolating yourself as a "loser," take a cue from these kids and look around. From cheerleading parents to hollering coaches, they use every ounce of help they can get to finish. The advantage these kids have that you may not is the group surrounding them.

Here's who you'll need in your tribe:

People to chase. These people are otherwise known as the people that have accomplished goals similar to yours. That couple with a killer marriage is a great resource when you're going through a rough patch. A woman who successfully started her business from scratch makes a great mentor when you're desperately trying to climb out of the red.

In these elementary school races, the middle school cross country kids volunteer to run ahead, with, and behind each student. This way, even the winner is chasing someone who is ahead and faster than them. You need someone who you can set your benchmark by. It's hard to predict the future, but learning from someone who has been where you're going is a great place to start.

People who help you keep pace. No one runs alone. You know what happens when you run alone? You break out fast and run out of steam. You can't keep up a breakneck speed, and eventually, you quit. So, you need to find a pace you can maintain long term.

In life, there are people at your same level. If you're a young mom, get around other young moms. If you're chasing a dream of becoming a c-level exec, you can learn just as much from the people around you as you can from those above you—this is where you refine the nuances of what you're doing. Find people at your level and spend time with them.

Iron sharpens iron, you know.

People to cheer you on. These are your helpers. Those people that hover at the finish line, clapping and screaming so loud that you set aside every ounce of fatigue to pump those arms and legs across that fucking finish line.

If you don't have a cheerleader in your life, get one. If you can't find one, be one.

Something opens up inside of us when we encourage others; we see things from a new angle and gather information from a different perspective. When we lift others, we rise.

&@#%$!

Humans were meant to be a part of a tribe. We are relational creatures who thrive off multiple fulfilling relationships. I used to use the excuse that, "I only have a few good friends. It's better that way." But as soon as someone told me the truth—that we're *made* to have multiple relationships to add to and fulfill multiple parts of our life, I never looked back. Now, I look for ways to get involved with people, even if I might get hurt—I set boundaries, remember? I know that every time I add a person to my life, I'm also adding a risk. Instead of writing off the whole of humanity because a handful of people hurt me in the past, I dive in and find the "good ones." I support them fiercely and I'm conscious of the energy they give back.

(P.S. They usually give more than I ever expect or anticipate. People are fucking incredible and I love them dearly. If you give more of them a chance, I think you'll find the same is true in your neck of the woods.)

For every person who tells you that you don't belong, there are four more waiting to embrace you because you do. Forget the one and find the four.

Now that you have your tribe…

Don't be an Asshat

Have you ever said something accidentally awful to someone? In the moment, maybe you think you're being funny or cleverly sardonic, but they don't get your humor and the comment comes out worse than intended? Oh man, I get myself in situations like that all the time and blame it on the exuberant amount of stand-up comedy my husband and I watch. I often "forget my audience" and wind up offending someone because they aren't the appropriate platform for my joke.

I'm the worst, however, and rarely realize I've fucked up until after. Then, I have to button up my big girl panties and go apologize. The other person is usually super kind and can look past my verbal stain to see my otherwise clean character. I've found that the times when I don't apologize don't work out well. Then, I end up feeling a new distance between us. Like that one time when I was, like, twenty, and I was taking a full bag of garbage to the dumpster at my coffee shop job. The giant black bag was jammed with wet, warm coffee grounds and it weighed 416 pounds, for sure. So I, in my ultimate immaturity, said, "What's the bag full of? Dead boyfriends?" For whatever weird reason, I thought my quip was funny. Except I said it in front of a coworker whose boyfriend had died several months earlier. And then, because I was immature in the way that I never knew what to do with my hands, I saluted her and *never apologized.*

Oh, things got awkward. And eventually, cold shoulders brushed each other near the espresso machine in mutual isolation.

Sometimes we can be asshats without realizing it or having the emotional maturity to fix it right away. Sometimes our poor behavior is truly the result of not knowing better. If you said something homophobic or racist out of ignorance, for instance, you don't have to classify yourself as a terrible person. Once you know better, do better. Don't keep feigning ignorance, because you're *not* just hurting yourself.

If you don't apologize for the intrusive, offensive, and painful things you say, the added tension could kill the relationship. Plus, not saying sorry is a dick move. That person we offended didn't know our intentions, and now they're almost looking to be offended again. Because we get what we look for—and because I still haven't mastered my tongue—it happens again, and eventually, there's no coming back. Trust me, it's way easier to say sorry.

Whether your intentions were pure and you apologize for your poor choice of words, or your intentions were bad and you truly meant the offense, you can own the sincerity and apologize, making steps to avoid a similar situation in the future. Instead of dwelling on the past, I let these memories fill me up with wisdom and I march forward into better friendships.

Okay, so I'm not really talking about the type of "asshat" that makes a mistake and apologizes. We all do that; it's called "being human." I'm talking about a deeper level of ass-hat-ness. Like, suck the life out of people, never-not-negative, taking others for granted all the time kind of asshat.

Please know, I'm not addressing anyone specifically when I say I've seen my fair share of asshats. We all have.

Don't be the asshole that yells at innocent strangers because you think it makes you look tough. If you've ever worked in customer service, you know who I'm talking about. The struggle is real, right? Those jerks shouldn't be allowed to have a cell phone with the damage they do with it daily… Then don't go around spouting toxic complaints about that asshole to everyone with ears.

Do you know what happens when we take out our aggressions on others? We give them our black eye.

If Eric from accounting snapped at you for asking him a simple question about your paystub, yeah that sucks. But then you snap at your kid when they want help with their homework. What the hell? Or you got a passive-aggressive text from your mother-in-law while in the Starbucks drive through, and you turn around and take it out on your barista, questioning her intelligence when she fumbles with your debit card. So not fair.

What if we let the buck stop with us? What if we stood secure enough in ourselves to shake off the shit of others (sound familiar?) without wiping it off onto others?

Let's be secure enough in our ability to emotionally handle a problem that we don't need to pass it on to everyone else.

So, if you can't keep a relationship alive, your friendships have all fallen apart, and even your doorman wants you dead, turn to the common denominator. Look in the damn mirror, you might be an asshat. It's possible that if the last ten people you interacted with never want to see your mug again, you're not being very awesome.

We are adults, and adults need filters.

And my goodness, can we please land within the lines at the grocery store. I've about had enough of people thinking it takes four spots to park a Buick. Do me a solid and remember that other people occupy this world.

Be the Friend You Want to Have

You're damn skippy I went there. You didn't think I'd get through a whole chapter on relationships and not recite the golden rule at least once, didja?

If we want to have good friends, we need to be a good friend. Again, common knowledge, yet not-so-common practice. I believe our lives are enriched by knowing and being in relationship with people. Even Jesus surrounded himself with a crew.

So, if we want others to pour energy into us, we need to give it right back. This isn't one-sided. It's the beauty of the ultimate human condition—our energy renews the more we share it, but we can't do this alone. Alone, our energy doesn't have anywhere to go. We're a cord without an outlet or vice-versa, and neither can illuminate the lamp without the other.

You should be aware of your limits, of course. Sometimes, you aren't able to drop everything and fly across the country to your college friend's side after she's been diagnosed with cancer. What can you do? Probably a lot more than you think.

If you can't be there for people on the bigger things, show up for the small stuff. Be on time when meeting your friends for brunch (or, do the best you can if you have an infant and spit up on your shoulder). Call people back with in an appropriate length of time when they leave you a message (totally raising my hand on this one).

And for sure, for *sure*, thank the people in your life. I want people to know I give a damn that they exist. I want to show others with my actions how much I appreciate them. Because if I don't show them how grateful I am for their presence in my life, they're going to start looking for appreciation elsewhere, and *that's* where true loneliness comes from.

Show gratitude to those who have contributed something to your life. If you've ever had a teacher, pastor, coach, leader, counselor, therapist, good friend or family member support you through a tough time, put down this book right now and go tell them thanks. Even if you've already done it, show them once more how their backing got you through. If someone poured into you in a way that deserves some thanks, write them a letter, call them, or better yet, arrange a time to treat them to dinner to express your gratitude. Too many times in life we take for granted these people who served us and helped us grow.

You can turn around and be rocket fuel to their soul with the simplest words of appreciation.

When someone gives, say thanks.

This also goes for taking graciously. If someone wants to do something special for you, let them. I *love* surprising people. I've had some of the best day dreams about jetting my husband away to a U2 concert to recreate our first date night after having kids. If I pulled it off and he up and didn't think he deserved to go and decided to stay home, it would crush me.

If someone wants to pay for your dinner, let them. If the neighbor boy wants to gift you with a mowed lawn—even if he won't make the lines straight—let him. Don't be a downer on someone's desire to give. Take graciously and, you guessed it, show your appreciation.

Do unto others, amiright?

FRAGILE
Pathetic Waste

No one can put away a burger like my older sister, Tara. No one. I have watched this chick and her ballerina figure scarf down a whole pizza with a bottle of Dr. Pepper and then slip a bikini on and rock the lake side, grooving to Ben Folds Five. It hardly ever seemed fair from the perspective of a teen like myself who had the self-imposed nickname of "Chunka-Lunka." I had to count the number of Oreos I shoveled down the hatchet while this brazen bitch could out-eat everyone at dinner and live to tell about it in her size zero jeans. (I called her that in the most loving yet jealous way possible.)

I, personally, never saw having a hot older sister as an issue until I was told as a teen that it was. Even though our parents did the best they could to keep us sheltered and blissfully ignorant about the mean world, comparison crashed into me all the same.

Everything around me screamed that I had to start knowing who I was, and no matter what personality type that took, I needed to be perfect doing it. From getting into the right activities at school so it would look good on my college application to fitting into the issued sizes in the dance squad at school, I learned in a hot second that I was being judged on what I did and how I looked doing it. I became insecure, and my relationship with Tara became strained. The fun and games of our childhood fell away, and we simply grew apart, each focusing on our own teen lives. But there was a lingering tension, at least on my end.

I was the first to be jealous that the boys looked at her instead of me, or that she got to shop the discounted mannequin-sizes for prom dresses while I had to pay full price for my size tens like every other Chunka-Lunka out there. She had baggage that went along with her looks, but when I was sixteen and felt like the Pumba to her Timon, I wanted what she had. At. All. Costs.

In hindsight, I'm very grateful that my "at all costs" didn't go as far as many others. Even though my journey to loving my body was on the mild end (no hospital visits, no long-term damage to my body), my starvation was strikingly traumatic. I remember making it three days once with only a few stalks of celery and an egg a day. When I ventured out with my

USING CURSE WORDS · 129

friends for a Friday night Christian hang at the coffee shop for our caffeine kick (Christian crack, folks), I could barely finish my child-sized vanilla latte because I was so worried about how much fat was in it. Yes, this was so long ago that we worried about the fat content in our milk. Thank God I've been blissfully drinking whole ever since.

The boy I dated at the time (not the one who became a ballerino; this guy loved Christian rock and wore a thick soul patch on his chin) was built like a Greek god. No, wait. My *husband* is built like a Greek god, this guy was more of the sixteen-year-old water boy of a Greek god, but you get the picture. He was beautiful, and he knew it. In fact, he once told me that he knew he was the more attractive one of us. Said it to my face, like, "Hey, you've been working on your body a ton lately, but I'm here to remind you I'm naturally better looking."

Instead of seeing my self-worth and telling this douche canoe to hit the highway, I made it my mission to live up to his standards. I dropped as much of my "baby fat" as I could living off celery and eggs, curbed my Oreo addiction, and I even started jogging in the mornings. (Y'all remember how much I hate running, right?) I pushed through the headaches I would get from dehydration (because water weighs some-thing) until I could borrow my sister's size zeros again. I became heavily Christian because he was—which is like being a regular Christian except your hands never leave the air when you worship, you use acronyms like "PTL" and "WWJD" in regular conversation, and you learn to gossip very carefully. "Megan's prayer request this week was epic. Y'all, we need to discuss it in great length, so we can pray for her accurately. It's what the Lord would want." And, as super Christians, we absolutely did not have sex, drink, or smoke. I was hell-bent on being the perfect girlfriend for this "perfect" guy.

I looked the part and acted the part, even pretending to like all the same music. Come on, we've all done it in our youth. You cannot tell me with absolute certainty that you were 100% honest when you told your high school boyfriend you too were totally into The Heavy Metal Kitten Project. *What a coincidence!*

One Monday, he dropped the hint that we might do a hot tub night at his house that Friday. He expected a few others to be there, so wandering Christian hands wouldn't be an issue. My parents gave me a tentative yes with the understanding that it was a group function, because how much trouble can a bunch of super Christians get into? It would be safe and fun.

But for me, knowing five days in advance that I'd be in a swimsuit in front of our youth group friends didn't seem like enough prep time. I needed to be flawless, so I could show our friends how amazing I was at being a trophy girlfriend so he'd "wife me up" someday and we'd have cute super Christian babies and live the perfect fairytale I knew I was destined for.

If I was going to be perfect, I needed every moment of that week. I ran every morning, became an expert dinner-shuffler so I could get away with taking fewer bites without my parents noticing, and did a hundred sit ups each night to make sure my stomach was flat. The look I was going for—the rail-thin, "probably shouldn't ride a wooden roller coaster for fear of fracturing a bone" look—came in one of two ways: naturally or painfully.

My sister got it naturally. I didn't.

Friday rolled around, and I spent too much time observing my hard work in the mirror before heading over. The roll on my stomach hadn't gone away, even with all the sit ups, so I practiced exactly how to suck in my gut without making it look like I was. I tucked the swimsuit around all the bits I thought made me imperfect, styled my hair and makeup in a way that I thought made me look like I cared but wasn't trying too hard, and I spritzed on a splash of musky body spray. The final look, to me, was cute, near-perfect, and at least three steps down from sexy, because I was more about showing how hard I'd worked on my body, not sending mixed signals.

I showed up, kissed the dude on the cheek, peeled off my clothes and dipped into the water in a seamless move that kept him from getting a good look at me. Then, we waited.

Not a soul showed up at my boyfriend's house. What should've been a violation of the fire code (I'm pretty sure his hot tub was only a four-seater and our group as at least eight strong) ended up feeling like an awkward double bath between two kids who only touched each other as awkwardly as humanly possible. While I hugged my knees to my chest to hide the "rolls" on my stomach, he fumbled with the disk in his cordless cd player. As soon as Skillet was blasting, out went the need for conversation. He began to act super nervous. I figured he hated that I couldn't say the right thing—why couldn't I be cool?—and I chided myself for being so awkward. He retreated inside to grab us some waters, tacked a note to the kitchen window overlooking the hot tub, and came back very satisfied.

I thought others were coming over that night, so I figured the note was for his friends who would waltz in at any minute and wonder where we were. "We're in the hot tub," I figured it read. "Come join us!"

But when he returned and slid in beside me, not across from me, I realized the note was probably more of a "sock on the doorknob" situation. I'd never been in a "sock on the doorknob" situation before, yet I'd seen the movies.

My heart knocked against my chest at the thought that this could turn into a make-out sesh. Just because my friends and I "swore an oath to our purities" didn't mean the lines didn't get blurred in one way or another, and I wasn't ready for that. At least, I didn't *think* I was. I also hadn't thought I'd ever give up Oreos and casserole with cheese just to look the way he wanted me to look. Maybe I was ready for this, I hadn't exactly made up my mind. Even so, this didn't seem the ideal situation to lock lips, not with the threat of neighbors seeing. No, no intimacy. For shit's sake, what if he tried to put his arm around my waist and felt my fat roll!

With the looming threat of physical contact hanging in the balance, a set of headlights traced along the fence, alerting us to a newcomer. *Thank God,* I thought, *friends!* The kitchen light was illuminated, the blinds were drawn, and the note was ripped off the window so fast I couldn't make out who was inside. I found out a hot second later when his dad thundered onto the patio.

"What's this?" his dad demanded, holding up the hand drawn note that I, too, read for the first time. In the quality penmanship of a teen in a hurry, it read:

Fuck off

"You weren't supposed to be home, Dad," the cowardly mound of chin hair beside me defended.

I sank as far into the water as I could.

"Yeah, well, *you're* supposed to be at youth group with your *male* friends. And why do you have your girlfriend over without anyone home?" his dad demanded.

And that's the moment my poor little teenage brain put it all together. There wasn't ever going to be anyone over. It wasn't okay with his parents that I was there because they didn't know; they were supposed to be otherwise occupied. The hot tub and Christian heavy metal were meant to "set the mood." (This is still very speculative, all these years later. Maybe he was going to try to mosh in the tub instead.)

As they fought, I took my cue and slunk out of the water, hiding into my towel and trying to put on my shoes as they argued.

As a parent, I now fully understand the rage felt by his dad, especially as he, too, saw for the first time the potential intentions of his son. I can imagine myself in the same situation with my kids, and I can't say I would've reacted differently… at least up until this next point, anyway.

What happened next left a seismic crack in my self-esteem for almost a decade.

As I fumbled to maintain my dignity, his dad turned around and looked down at the towel I clutched to my chest. Turning back to his son, the man said, "What were you two planning on doing?"

Two? I had no part in this, sir. But I couldn't get the words out of my celery-hole. Instead, I just watched the soap opera before me, horrified I was connected to it.

"Nothing," my ever-suave boyfriend yelled. "Gosh, Dad. Leave us alone. I'm old enough to do what I want."

His dad was making hand gestures by now, angrily tossing his outstretched hand between us like he was directing traffic. "I thought you were going to take your purity ring seriously."

"I am, Dad. Stay out of my business."

"Until you're old enough to join the military, your business is *my* business."

"I'll never join the military! I'll never even wear a suit, and I know that's all you want from me. You won't even take my music seriously."

"I'm not trying to force your life right now." His dad shook his head, flabbergasted, still gesturing with his hands. "I'm just trying to keep you from getting your girlfriend pregnant."

"We weren't going to have sex, Dad. Get a grip."

"Even if you weren't planning, it probably would've happened," he insisted.

"How do you know that? You don't know anything."

"Son," his dad barked with a final hand gesture directed at me, giving me a complete head-to-toe glance of disgust, "you wouldn't even be tempted to have sex if you kept *better company*."

(I'll pause here, so you can stop gasping and let go of those pearls you're clutching. Take a deep breath, in and out. Better now?)

Yup. It happened just like that. Before I was comfortable driving on the highway or old enough to vote, I was made to feel like I was "asking for it" by my boyfriend's dad.

In my quest to become the perfect girlfriend, I had become the perfect temptation. And upon realizing my title, it was clear that I was also supposed to feel shameful about it. Everything I'd worked so hard for rewarded me with shame. And, since I already had eating issues to begin with, I slammed these two together like a strong-ass magnet and spent the next decade of my life wanting to look good but feeling horrible about it.

Many of us have struggled with a personal tale of humiliation. Some people shove it down until the festering wound comes out in other areas of their life, while others tackle the problem head-on, and become very *Stella Got Her Groove Back* about it, demanding better for their lives.

I did neither of these things. I, like many others, let someone else's perception of me shape who I was. I took all the shame from that night— which I can now see I *never* had a part in deserving—and I let it become part of my identity. I figured I *was* asking for it. After all, I was the one who wanted to look perfect. If I had remained chunky, I probably would've worn a suit that covered me more, and when his dad came home, he may not have seen me as a threat. I would've just been his son's chubby friend. (Again, speculation.)

His accusation about my intentions didn't keep the starvation away, and it got worse before it got better. The way I looked to others became a very fragile topic. I became thinner, but I covered up. His dad still took out his insecurities on me—little sixteen-year-old me—several more times, and even met with my parents about how I shouldn't be allowed to be alone with boys. Yes, that happened. My parents, bless their amazing hearts, refused to put up with that type of control and said some badass words in return that I won't repeat here.

Even so, I didn't know better, I plummeted into a sea of self-pity and starvation, feeling like I'd caused all of this.

Although I never became so thin that I needed medical intervention, I destroyed myself on the inside, believing the way I looked was the most important thing about me.

Years went by when I'd wake and my first thought was about how much I'd eaten the day before. My mental food tally dictated how good I felt about myself before I even unrolled the covers. My personal worth was wrapped around a scale, and since it never seemed good enough, I became very fragile. Not just my bones, but my soul.

When I think back on the brainpower I wasted counting calories and obsessing over workouts, I get nauseous. I could've gotten a master's degree with all that energy. Instead, I toggled for a decade between being proud of my body and being afraid anyone would see it and think I was "asking for it." Not much changed in ten years, other than the slight variance between the people I dated and the diets I went on. Still, the pain was always there like I was made of glass.

Enter my husband. When Nick came into my life, he was nearing the end of his 30s while I hovered in my mid-20s. Not only did this match us well on the maturity scale, but it also gave him an edge over the competition. At his age, my now-husband wasn't interested in vanity. He never said shit like, "You're wearing *that* to go out?" or "Have you thought about how that outfit makes you look?" (both things I was used to hearing on the regular). Nick ran his hands over my rolls like he never wanted to let them go.

He never once made a negative comment about my appearance. Trust me, I've been hyper-aware of it for most of my life and would've known, even if it was just implied. It took a long time for me to get healthy, fully, and build strength in my body-love. My husband told me he loved the way I looked, and then he proved it by watching me make, grow, and naturally birth three healthy-sized babies. He loved me through the aftermath of each pregnancy as if I was still his Jessica Rabbit—and if you've given birth, you know that's the part where you suffer from feeling like a still-large, deflated balloon whose insides have turned inside-out. He ran his hands over my squishy, deflated belly in awe of what it housed, and kissed my never-washed, new mom hair. And when a man loves a woman like that, she doesn't give a fuck how she looks.

And although Nick's support and love helped me overcome my fragile state, I wasn't healed through him alone. I had a come-to-Jesus moment with myself during my first pregnancy. I saw just how fragile I had let myself become and I wanted to set a better example for my kids.

I can now say with certainty that I love my body. In fact, if you know me now, you'd probably be shocked to read this story. I have more body confidence than most people. This temple made three kids, helped me show my husband just how much I love him, and has been my constant companion.

It's the only body I'll ever get, and I look down at my rolls and dark arm hair and sun-spotted skin with amazement. I love every jiggle, every dimple of cellulite, every silver hair and I even love the precancerous patch of cells on my back because they taught me to slow down.

I feed my body well and perform my favorite activities of yoga and snowboarding with verve because working out is no longer about burning calories and suffering through vomit-inducing high activity. Everything I do to myself now, I do because I love my body, not because I hate it.

If you don't love your body, I encourage you to start. It can be one of the most fulfilling relationships you'll ever have. I'd totes run through town in my undies if it helped people be comfortable with themselves.

Even with my self-love, the lesson wasn't quite learned. I had some repairing to do.

Tara may have grown up with her gorgeously natural dancer's figure, and with it was blessed to perform on some of the greatest stages. However, in addition to her God-given gifts and the physique to match, she also suffered through constant flare ups of fibromyalgia, IBS, and anxiety that caused her to finish her senior year of high school at home. She had boys break her heart just like I did. She had struggles and fears and lived her own version of being fragile.

More than my disappointment over spending a decade obsessed with how I looked, I feel a deep loss for all the time I could've spent building Tara up instead of obsessing about myself. When I think of all the times Tara and I could've been laughing together over one of our inside jokes, but instead I was going on an emergency run so I wouldn't have a fraction of an inch hanging over my belt, I want to cry. If I had taken my eyes off my own fragile state long enough to see how much pain she was in, I could've helped her talk through it. We could've built more memories and championed each other.

She's always been my best friend. I can't say I was always hers. I let my selfishness keep me from helping her, and I regret that. It wasn't my fault that an insecure man made an unfair judgment about me, leaving a deep scar. However, it was my choice to be identified by his idea of me and not by my own truth. It wasn't my choice to be fragile, but it was my choice to remain fragile.

So, what did I learn from this?

Consider that your situation may be happening *for* you, not *to* you. I won't lie, I want to throw up in my mouth saying this one because it's *so* not what I wanted to hear when I was feeling fragile. Since the potential results are more important than getting uncomfortable for a second, I say we go for it. Even when things happen to you, it helps to view the situation through a more constructive lens. Even if something bad happened to you (gulp!) you can still grow from it, finding the lesson and how you can make the hurt work *for* you. It doesn't make it easier, and it won't make it hurt less (at least not immediately), but by becoming stronger through your struggle instead of being weakened by it, you get to be the master of your life again. I don't know about you, but when given the choice, I try to always choose to be strengthened rather than weakened. Maybe that's just me, though?

Don't compare struggles. Just because someone looks great doesn't mean they feel awesome, too. People struggle in ways you and I can't see.

Get your ice princess on and let it go. Whatever you want is probably on the other side of your white-knuckled grasp. There is so much beauty in letting go. The harder I clung to my idea of what a perfect body looked like, the less I loved my body. As soon as I realized how amazing my body always had been, the self-love came back and did its healing work. If you loosen your grip around the hurt you've been carrying around for years, you may find the very thing you thought that hurt would fix will come to you. Then it's your job to figure out what to do with it. Lessons, remember?

This world can be cruel. We can find "mean" anywhere we look, and the world doesn't need any more of it. Be kind. I'm not suggesting this horrid epidemic of body shaming is an easy fix, but I'm pretty sure the answer isn't isolation and silence.

Instead...

Talk to your pain. It's real. It cries out because it wants your attention. Shoving your pain to the back corner won't make it go away. Ignoring pain turns it into a festering monster, which is harder to deal with. And if you never deal, your pain monster will go to your grave with you in the form of bitterness, resentment, limitations, fears, or (still) a searing anguish as if the event just happened yesterday. Get in a safe place (with safe people if you need support) and spend some time unpacking your pain. Look at it in a raw and unbiased light, and then…

Release it. Understand that it happened to you. Whether it was a name you were called, a behavior which held you captive, an idea or fear you let turn into something bigger than your dreams, you can allow your mind to reorganize the memory into wisdom. Like my pastor once so lovingly improvised from the pulpit one Sunday not too long ago, "Stop patting pain on the back like it belongs in your life."

Replace it. If you can, replace a bad emotion with a good one. Every time I resolved to just forget about my negative body image, it always trickled back in because I never filled the hole with anything positive. I didn't ditch my destructive weight fluctuation until I decided to love my body, and then I treated it like I loved it until I believed that I did. I had to replace my shame and physical disdain with an equally strong emotion, and I choose love because this life is *way* too short to care about a few pounds, and this world is way too mean not to be proactive. Finally…

Upgrade. My ultimate fix came from upgrading to a man mature enough to make me feel beautiful by loving me (and my body) for who I already was. My husband doesn't just find me attractive, he loves where my body can take us. His perspective shift helped cement mine, and though I could've found a love for my body without him, I wouldn't have found it in a cycle of bad relationships. Whatever you keep doing on a loop— dating shallow guys, keeping friends who put you down, your enduring involvement with the mean mom group at the park—maybe it's time to upgrade to the kind of person who will hold you in your fragility, instead of swinging bats at you while you're down. It wasn't until a few years into my marriage that I truly saw how badly my patterns affected me. And although my diamond in the rough husband can't be shared—sorry ladies—you can upgrade too. There are amazing people in this world who are looking for amazing people like you. The new relationship/ friendship/environment won't fix the problem; you must do that. But staying with someone who hurts you emotionally or physically won't get you any closer to the fix either.

It isn't wrong to have feelings, even feelings of being fragile, but it's dangerous when those feelings have you. You may not be in a place where you love yourself enough to say, "I'm worth more than this pain." Keep drowning your insecurities with love and find others to support you in the same. Soon, you'll wonder why you let those pains hurt you for so long.

&@#%$!

If you're stuck feeling fragile—if you're the 22-year-old me with tears rolling down your cheeks about how "horrible your life is" because of the mean thing a douche canoe said to you five years ago—there's an important piece about your pain we need to talk about. Some people in your life would never say what I'm about to say next because they don't want to make your fragileness worse by adding guilt. Yet I refuse to shy away from the truth because it this the *final* thing that helped me release the last of my hurts…

Your pain hurts others.

Yup. Reread that as many times as you feel necessary. Hate me if you want to; I'll take the fall for it, so your loved ones don't have to be the bad guy here.

Do you know how many times my hurts prevented me from being a good mom? Do you know how many times my husband has had to say the same positive things to me over-and-over again to try to scribble out the words some d-bag once told me? Can you imagine how many people I could've helped with my words if I hadn't let that one editor's notes fester in my mind about my writing being garbage? Can you imagine the impact I could've had on others going through the same body image shit if I hadn't been so fucking glued to the bathroom scale?

I know I added to the pain of others by perpetuating my own.

When we're hurting, we don't always see the pain we cause others. When we're fragile, we don't recognize the effect of our actions because we're being (dare I say) selfish. Okay, before you get your panties twisted, yes, I spend most of this book advising you to *be* selfish—to concentrate on yourself so that you can live your best damn life. But the dangerous side of selfishness is that it can keep you detached from reality and drag others with you. Don't take your pain and dribble it out into every interaction you have, totally unaware that you're dragging others down with you.

So what if that lady flipped you off when you passed her? Don't take it out on the next person who cuts you off. Who cares if Karen from accounting doesn't like you? Don't neglect all the people who *do* like you because you're so busy complaining about why one person doesn't.

Be a river, not a cesspool. Let emotions pass through you; acknowledge them and learn from them, and then let them go, so you have room for even more greatness.

You can be defined by something bigger than your hurt. You, and only you, get to define yourself. That's hard to swallow when you've been defining yourself by curse words your whole life: bad choices, fears, hurts, and self-pity. You CAN be defined by something greater. If you only have a tiny bit of energy left and you've been wondering how to spend it, reinvest it on yourself. Give yourself what you need to begin rebuilding that strength, and let people come alongside you who care about you enough to help.

Letting go of your past pains isn't magic, but once you've done it, it certainly feels like it is.

A Special Note:

This is hard shit, right? Thus far, our hurt has kept us "safe." It's hard to release old pains when they seem to exist as a reminder not to get hurt again.

Being fragile doesn't actually keep us safe though, does it? Our self-preservation-oriented brains convince us that we're safe inside our fragile state, so we retreat further into ourselves. As long as we don't break the boundaries we've created—as long as we do everything exactly the way our fragile hearts need—we'll be okay.

Unfortunately, bad shit happens.

Just in case you don't feel safe outside of your fragile state, this part is for you:

You are NOT dirty.

It is NOT your fault.

You CAN overcome the hurt and move forward.

And, in case you need to hear this—and my prayer is that if this is you, these words resonate: The quickest way to separate yourself from people who cause you pain is to GET THEM OUT OF YOUR LIFE.

Obviously, this isn't always possible with exes with whom you share custody or coworkers or some other situations, but you *can* work around those limitations and find a safe place to be. You have full control over how people treat you because you train them to treat you either well or poorly. I know, I know. This is horrible to hear right now, yet boundaries are vital.

If you need help, look around for a loving person who can be your hands and voice for a while.

It's okay to feel hurt. It doesn't mean you're broken or weak, it doesn't mean you aren't living life to your fullest potential, and it doesn't mean that if you "fix" your life, you won't hurt anymore. Like many other curse words, our "hurt" can be controlled and managed. But preventing hurt takes a diligent practice of setting up and adhering to boundaries, managing expectations, and giving yourself grace.

This is life. Although we can help prevent the way we react to how others treat us, this doesn't mean we can always prevent being victimized. Yes, you can change your environment so your chances of getting hurt are drastically decreased, but you can't prevent all types of victimization. Put preventative measures in place and understand that no matter what, it isn't your fault.

And once again for those in the back:

You weren't "asking for it."

AFRAID
Scared Shitless

I am not afraid of bees. I think it's important to clarify that from the start, even if I learned one of my greatest lessons this year while running from a swarm of them.

Also, to be fair, these weren't the pollinating-type of honey bees that our world will soon be in short supply of. And they weren't the sweet little bumbles, obvi. In the spring, a queen paper wasp told her crew to set up shop in one of our eves. And, because the drone bugs follow whatever the queen says—or however that works with paper wasps—they weren't going anywhere. I tried a whole bottle of bug spray on them. Though the "extra strength" pesticides caused them to stumble, I swear it just made the wasps stronger.

I've read too many articles about the dangers of insecticides and figured that the more I sprayed, the more I increased the likelihood that my children would ingest the poisons and grow an eleventh toe or something. Plus, if one can of chemicals hadn't annihilated them, who knows what two cans would do. I could be staring down the barrel of a superbug epidemic in my front yard, and that seemed avoidable.

So, I took to the hose. Every morning, I loaded the kids into the van to go to the gym, library, park, playdate, whatever I was doing to stay sane during the hundred-day boot camp of parenting that is summer. Every day, I'd turn on the car and AC, and take a moment to go full-Rambo on the wasps' nest. Just the right jet of water at just the right pressure blasted off whatever the wasps could build the day before.

It became a daily habit to spray down the wasps, so their hive and population wouldn't grow out of control and endanger my kids. But the habit of dissuading them from permanent residence soon became a pleasure as I morbidly enjoyed the wet *flump* that the loosened mass of nest made when it hit the dirt.

Relentlessly, they remained, chronically rebuilding their paper hive just moments after I'd sprayed down the remains of what they'd just built. I'll admit, their commitment to the build—and probably to appeasing their queen—was admirable. No matter how many times I knocked down the feeble attempt to grow a hive of doom, they kept trying. It started getting to me emotionally, and I had to force myself to remember that story the beekeeper at last year's county fair told me about how a group of wasps murdered her honey bees. They would just set up their hives in the nearby trees and then wait until the vital, majestic honey bee exited the hive; then the horrible, nightmare-inducing wasps of death would attack and pluck off their sweet, brown cousins.

Horrifying right? This is what I was up against; it was the battle I was currently losing.

I should've also started this story with a preface that I have no green thumb whatsoever. Well, it's too late now, so let's keep going...

My mom studied horticulture and has blessed our family with an abundance of organically grown vegetables, herbs, and gorgeous flowers for as long as I can remember. I inherited none of that. In contrast to her amazing abilities, I have the impressive talent of killing houseplants in record time. Unlike my wasp-killing abilities, I've murdered cacti with ease (and way less water).

I've since gotten better and patted myself on the back just the other day for keeping six mini-houseplants alive on the windowsill. They, too, had a rough start when I left them outside the day I bought them. The deer came and ate the greens off them because I live in a town where the deer think my lawn is their own personal toilet. Y'all think it's cute—it's annoying. Anyhow, I nursed these little plants back to life, and now they're doing great. I think I'll graduate to a potted palm soon.

So, I've always thrown my hands in the air and said, "Welp, as long as our lawn is mowed and trimmed, and as long as I pull most of the weeds, so I don't look completely neglectful, that's good enough for me."

Our flowerbeds had little in them when we moved into our home a few years ago—a couple of plants you'd think were dead from the outside. Then my mom visited, and she brought along her horticultural wisdom. She took one look at my lilac tree and claimed it officially *not* dead. "Just put the hose on a steady, low stream. Then stick the nose of the hose directly on the base of the tree for an hour. It just wants a long, deep drink of water," she told me.

Sure enough, I did what she said, and tiny purple buds came out. But, without a steady habit of going into the yard to perform this task, the blossoms were short lived. Not much of what remained of the garden was truly dead; it just needed to be watered.

How funny would it be if I told you there was a dead rose bush under the exact spot where the dumb wasps built their endless charade of torture? Welp, settle into the hilarity because that's exactly what happened. You've probably guessed the results by now. Every day of blasting down the hive, I was also watering a very beautiful bush of neon pink roses. In the time it took to convince the hive to pack up once and for all, I had watered this incredible bush back to life.

In my trial of eradicating a group of pests, I found beauty.

I can't say I would go out and plant a dozen more rose bushes, though I might. Or, I'll just keep my modest collection of houseplants alive. Either way, I learned a very important lesson from those bees, the ones I was never afraid of: sometimes all it takes to ignite (or reignite) a dream is a problem. If I'd never felt at war with a hive of wasps that didn't want to take a watery "no" for an answer, I never would've been blessed with splashes of neon pink in my front yard. Sure, it wasn't much, but once I started watering the lilac tree again (regularly) and the lavender, and even the little orange lily I found around the Fourth of July, our flowerbeds filled.

More than that, I found a new habit that I loved—taking a few minutes out of my crazy publishing schedule every day to water the garden. Either before work, during a break in the middle of the day, or spraying out a gentle mist of hose water into the yellow patches of grass at dusk, I found my peaceful place. I flooded my flowerbeds with color—okay, *flood* maybe isn't the right word when it comes to my flowers; it wasn't that full—but what I really did was deluge my busy mind with peace. For those ten minutes a day, I slipped my toes out of my heels and pressed them into the grass, wetting my fingers with water and splashing my pant hem with mud.

No, it wasn't much. My little garden didn't change the world or make my business more profitable. It didn't even pay me back with veggies or rosemary, though I was able to pluck a few sprigs of lavender to keep in a satchel in my underwear drawer like a real fucking grown up. No, all my garden did was make me happy.

It made me happy.

Now, happiness is subjective. To most of us happiness is something we reach for in intervals but only feel occasionally. We're "happy" when we get a promotion, "happy" when we get a new throw pillow set, "happy" when our friends remember our birthday. When queried though, how many of us say we're happy every day? There are plenty of Suzy Sunbeams who can find a ray of joy in any situation. But we're talking about miserable, pre-revelation Myra here. I hadn't been happy in months. I'd let the troubles of life become my identity. I hadn't smiled in so long I forgot what it felt like to curl my lips without forcing it for a photo.

A rose bush might seem like just a freaking rose bush to you. To me, at the time of deep tribulation in my crumbling life, these flowers were a beacon of hope. When the flower petals unfurled, I saw a sliver of beauty in a place I once only saw sticks. And if that could be true for a plant, perhaps it could be true for my soul.

Maybe all I needed to do was water the plant I wanted to grow. If I wanted my business relationships to blossom with opportunity, I needed to water those relationships. If I wanted to become a better writer, I needed to put my energy into writing. If I wanted to be a better leader to my team, I needed to start by slowing down enough to see what they needed support with. If I wanted to have more sex with my husband, I needed to help make that happen.

Look, in hindsight, all of this seems fundamental. And from the outside, I'm sure you're all, "Fucking duh, Myra" by now. But remember, I was afraid of stopping because if I wasn't working, I wasn't moving, and if I wasn't advancing, I wasn't pursuing my dream. I was convinced forcing that dream into existence was the only thing that would make me happy. Instead, it made me very Clark Griswold-y, gritting my teeth and forcing a gigantic Christmas tree into my living room to *force* a happy holiday into existence. If you're a National Lampoon fan, you know nothing good comes from forcing shit to happen.

By now, you're probably wondering why I didn't choose a terrifying tale for my chapter on fear.

"Why didn't she talk about the financial crisis she created in her household by opening a high-risk company with no experience?"

"Why didn't she discuss the threat of gun violence and the current political climate and the fear of raising children in a world where we have to worry about cyberbullying and suicide?"

"Why is she talking about stupid wasps and roses?"

Dear sisters, we can't fix the big fears if we don't fix the little ones. How the hell are you going to perform open heart surgery on yourself if you're too afraid to give yourself a couple stitches? How was I going to "grow my flowers" if I didn't have bees to run from? And yes. Even though I wasn't afraid of wasps *at the start,* I became very not-not-afraid of them when they started swarming me that one time when I didn't set the hose to the "jet" setting. In the seconds it took me to realize I was trying to blast them away with a gentle mist, the devil bugs turned on me. I fumbled with the hose attachment for a terrifying moment, attempting to arm myself with a better spray, but they bombed toward me too fast and

I abandoned my post (and my kids in the car, not my best moment) by running across the lawn toward safety. I didn't get stung, but what a nightmare.

And maybe that's a good point, too. I wasn't afraid of wasps before. I didn't like them, but I wasn't afraid of them. Just because a fear is new and doesn't present itself early on doesn't mean it's not valid. We grow and change, and our fears do too. Even if a fear is new—and you *will* grow new fears before the end of your life—doesn't mean it needs to overtake you. I wasn't afraid of those yellow demon spawn before, and I definitely had bigger fears to face, though I was still committed to dealing with them. Because if I didn't, how was I going to handle the big stuff?

We all have our big fears, and they're valid. It takes action and devotion to overcome the whopper fears. But being afraid my kids would get stung and fearing rejection in the publishing industry (and life, let's be honest) are just varying degrees of the same bullshit fear that something bad was going to happen.

Perhaps your big fear is that you'll wind up alone while all your friends get married and have kids without you. Or you're a single mom, and you've been hurt before, and you have a list of fears that are all working against you.

Maybe your big fears are that you'll never reach your goals before you die. The world has beat you down, and the drought of your dreaming "garden" has been so severe that you figure abandoning it is the only way to proceed. So, you bulldoze the flowerbed and fill it in with rocks instead.

Surely, you can take care of a rock. Except, that's not going to fulfill you if visions of roses still dance in your head.

Or you do the opposite: you dig in, refusing to give up this desert landscape of your dream—this thing you've always wanted to do—but of course you started too late, don't have an edge, and can't compete.

You have a valid dream, no matter what your garden looks like. It just requires action.

Maybe you're like me and always wanted to be a published author. You wrote and queried for years, only to receive polite passes and general indifference from the community around you. Save for the support of a few loyal writing friends, I clawed my way into a better understanding of what made writing work. This took years. Let's not talk about how many, it's embarrassing.

Then, I discovered that I could edit better than I could write and let that become an excuse to abandon my own work. I listened to the "expert" opinions in my life and switched the course of my race to reach a different finish line. Don't feel bad for me, it's an awesome excuse. I've edited several award-winning books and guided the publication of many more. As much as I hate to admit it, I felt comfortable giving my best to books that weren't my own because, no, I wouldn't get the glory, but I also wouldn't get the bad reviews. My contribution was enough since it piggy-backed on the accomplishments of others, and I had little tie to the outcome.

Yeah, it was a shallow as it sounds, but listen; I wasn't hurting anyone but me. I gave my best to each book I edited, and they reflected it. I never cut corners. producing the highest-quality work I could, contributing to award-winning work, which is pretty badass. (Do you hear that, Myra circa 2017? What you've done is badass!)

Yet for myself? I wanted to get the "okay" from an outsider before I rekindled my dreams of writing and publishing my work. I was quick to affirm the work of others and pursue it with everything I had (financial investment included) but wasn't willing to sit with my own fears of rejection for ten minutes to get a half-page typed.

My big fear, the whopper fear I needed to deal with over time, was that my writing would never be good enough; that without the backing of an editorial cheerleader, it wasn't okay for my "okay" to be okay.

After all the rejections I'd received (several hundred over many years, if I haven't mentioned that already) I dressed up my fears in selfless clothing and presented them as a "sacrifice for the dreams of others."

What about my dreams? What about the whole reason I opened this company, the only reason I lost sleep and a social life and general hygiene for all those years of writing at odd hours to practice my craft? What about my writing?

Sure, I could help others all day and find fulfillment in the task, but without pursuing this final piece of my literary dreams, the joy of editing turned into an act of resentment. I'd sit down to work on someone else's manuscript with a grumble that I wish I was working on my own. My resentment grew out of control as the demands of those around me heightened. I couldn't do enough work fast enough and well enough. I was chronically exhausted, putting my energy into things without seeing the return. I lost sight of my "why."

I forgot that I wanted to affect people with *my* words, too.

I forgot what it was like for my soul to ignite when my fingers flew on the keyboard.

I forgot what my dream felt like. And forgetting, I discovered, was scarier than my fear that my writing wasn't good enough. At the end of the day, my writing would never be good enough for everyone. It could've always gone through another round of edits. I could've spent a few extra years on my craft before putting my work out there. Nevertheless, I'm not going to let the excuse that I'm "not good enough" keep me in a shameful place of perpetual fear. If I didn't get my words out now, I never would. If I waited until it was "good enough," future-me probably wouldn't think it was good enough either. I'd table my book again.

I can't guarantee this book will be a bestseller, but I *can* guarantee it's better than anything I've pumped out yet. You know how I know this? This isn't my first fucking book.

I have a half-dozen nearly publishable manuscripts gathering cyber dust on my hard drive. At least two of those could've made it into print. They might've been successful, or they may have only sold to my friends and family. But because I couldn't see past what they could've been—a best-seller, duh, I just need to put 800 more hours into each of them to make them *perfect*—then what was the point? I only had top-notch dreams for these books. I was convinced they were never good enough to match the super-duper-high-caliber-work needed to hit the bestseller category. No matter how much I worked on them, I could only see where I still failed. So, instead of trying a few different angles to get them published, I gave up.

Guess what, chicken butt: those books aren't doing me any good sitting on my computer. Well, unless you count them as beautiful lessons learned—which I do, of course. Sure, they've done me good, yet that's where they stopped. Those books can't be someone's new favorite story while camped out on my hard drive.

And this one? This book in your hand right now could be challenged, tweaked, and perfected, but it's published. I'll find faults in it after it's printed in stone… er, um, paper. From what I've heard, most authors find faults in their work after publication anyway. It doesn't matter; it's *in the world* because I'm not letting my big fears win anymore. I won't let my fear of not being good enough win and take me through round after round after round of edits just to sit on my laptop with the rest of the manuscripts.

Yes, I'm putting this hot piece of garbage out into the world before it's "ready," because it isn't a hot piece of garbage and it *is* ready for the right person. The rest of the bullshit is just my fear talking.

My fear is also saying that if I don't get it out there, I'll never find that my work is "good enough" because I'll have no benchmark to gauge it against. I'll never know if a principle in this book changed the life of one reader in time to cheat the lies that keep us stuck.

Even if this book isn't perfect, the next one I put out might be closer. I'll always get better, improve my craft, and I'll never give up again.

I want my moment of happiness.

And you know what? It's worth every potential sting (wasp or bad review). It's worth all those times I grumbled watering the wasps or fighting my fear of rejection. It's worth it, because my fears are valid, but so are my dreams.

The wasps built, and still, I watered. Still, I remained diligent to the charge. Still, I wrote a book.

Now, it's Autumn. No amount of watering can bring the roses back to life for a while, not with the overnight temperatures and daily frost. I get a break from watering, but now it's nature's turn to contribute its warm paint collection on every leaf overhanging the streets. The flowers will come back, and when they do, I will water them again. Wasps or no wasps.

It's Autumn now. This book is printed, and it will either find a fan base or it could only fulfill my dream of being out there. I'll keep "watering" my writing. Wasps or no wasps.

There's a lot I could say about fear; how to overcome it, what to look for, how to make it work for you. And I promised you a book full of advice, so I'll give you a few nuggets here. The important thing to know about fear is it won't go away. Either it will grow, it will fade, or you will change and ditch it. I don't know about you, but I don't want to leave fear unchecked, to either grow or fade. I'll blast that wasp nest every time and watch my roses grow.

Fear Shmear...

It's my experience that our fears overwhelmingly stem from one of three general areas: loss, hardship, and outcome. Sometimes, it's a wicked fear that avalanches from all sides, but usually, there's a singular hang up. To make matters worse, we tend to gravitate toward the same fears on repeat. There's good news in that fun fact: if each of your fears has the same root, you only have one root to pull out.

It's as easy as you make it.

Fear of Loss

Big one, right?

Instead of letting the fear of loss hit you in the gut before the loss has happened, shift your focus on what you can gain instead. We're going to lose things: money, relationships, and loved ones. Life is liquid and flows in chaotic ways. We can't control loss, but we can focus on what can be gained—understanding, wisdom, experience, a better way for next time.

Fear of Hardship

"This is going to take *for-EVER!* This process is going to suck."

That's me talking about almost every part of my business when I opened it. Setting up my website, opening an LLC, paying taxes. I felt the hardship of a new task before I ever needed to perform it. I still do this sometimes—no one is perfect. I'll look at improving the system to a necessary part of my business and wish I could run away and be a wild-boy like Mowgli from the Jungle Book. *Fuck this shit, I'm out.* I want to scream at what's in store for me.

And you know what? Most of the time, the horrid task I spend hours dreading takes me less energy and work than I thought. Yup, it's usually *easier* than anticipated. Even if it is a hard task, the fear and worry only makes it worse.

Instead, I try to focus on the positive. What can I learn from this? What new skill can I pick up? How can I make the process fun and enjoyable? How can I make the process easy?

It's as easy/fun/educational as we make it, right?

Fear of Outcome

Most of us have a "What if you do X and it doesn't result in Y?" question circling in our mind.

"What if I give my book everything and no one likes it?"

"What if I try to spice up my relationship by seducing my spouse and I just feel silly for trying something new?"

"What if I go back to school for four years and I still can't find a job in my desired field?"

Here's one… What if you don't try?

Can we readjust the "what ifs," please?

What if you do the thing and it *works?*

What if you do your best and let go of the outcome completely? What if God has a promise for you waiting on the other side of your fear, but you have some lessons to learn before you can realize that promise?

Be a visionary for your life. Design the world around you and decide which parts of it to be active about.

Stop letting your fears dictate your actions. Because, I'm sorry dear sisters, there's only one way to get over your fears for good, and that's with action.

What dream have you been putting off because you're "too afraid?"

What action can you do now—right *now*—to take you one step closer to achieving your dream?

Stop reading and go do it. You can pick up where you left off, go ahead and dogear the page. I promise not to be offended.

OVERWHELMED
Fucking Screwed

My hard drive crashed last fall.

A year into starting up my publishing company, I ran my entire business from this computer. All my files, manuscripts, graphics, systems, logins—everything was lost. Not to mention the more important things—family photos, videos, scribbles of poetry, and future book outlines. After three opinions and seven weeks of bustling my broken eBaby around town, the diagnosis was clear: pay a few grand and *maybe* get some of the content recovered. Even after I paid the bill, a cure wasn't guaranteed.

I swallowed the news, hobbling together what I could from the Cloud, Google drive, email (thank you email), and a copy of the computer's contents I had backed up a few months before on an external hard drive. I didn't save it all, though it was enough to start over.

My husband, ever the gadget guy, saw a silver lining in my catastrophe and eagerly went looking for a replacement. My husband loves, capitol L-O-V-E-S shopping for electronics. I don't give a damn—so he does the shopping. We work well together like that.

He called me from his perch in the laptop department of Best-Husband-Ever R Us (that's a totally legit, trademarked name, you know) and rattled off a list of features, rams, gigs, decibels, frogs, all that jazz.

I'll be honest, I tuned most of it out. I didn't care what brand, what stats, or if one was a few bucks cheaper than the other. All I cared about was how soon I could use it and get my company up and running again. So instead, I used the phone-equivalent of a bored nod, "Uh huh. Mmhmm. Oh. Ah. Sure. No. Hmm. Ahh."

We went on like this for a good bit until he stopped and said, "Sorry, I can tell you don't really care about the details, so I'll make it easy."

Finally, I thought, *I don't speak computer.*

He continued, "Option A is less likely to implode if you have too many tabs open."

"That's the one I want, then."

"It's more money…"

"I don't care. Buy it."

(To be fair, I didn't buy it with the phantom piles of cash I had lying around. We put it on credit like hot-blooded consumers on the fast-track to suffocating debt. Even though it was a blessing for me to be able to do that in the first place, I don't endorse you to do the same without at least putting some thought into it. I clearly didn't, which just goes to show how much I couldn't wait to stop being overwhelmed by computers and start being overwhelmed by my forty open tabs again.)

Why did I want the computer so bad and, like, *now*? Because I was overwhelmed with not being overwhelmed. You can insert as much nervous laughter as you want here, I can take it.

I was the queen of overwhelm. I wish I were saying that in a cutesy, self-deprecating way, but that wasn't the case. I'm not "passing through a coffee drive-thru at 2 pm because I was up late" kind of overwhelmed. That's adorable. I wish that were me. I was more like "OMG, Myra, are you *okay?* You look dead. Sorry, that was mean, but really. Are you running out of white blood cells or something?" kind of overwhelmed.

The load I piled on my plate didn't just keep me "up late" once a week to stay caught up. I took on three full-time jobs worth of work. I committed to something in January, and it wouldn't even get touched until I was on spring break (correction, until my family was on spring break while I worked in the hotel room), and that's only if I could perform thirty straight twelve-hour workdays on top of my day job and taking care of my family.

I wish what I used to try to cram into a day was a cute mess of "I have this index card *full* of todos." Instead, my "Master To-Do List" was twelve pages long, typed and single-spaced. I once showed the list to a work colleague, and she laughed. "That looks like our company schedule to a week-long event with a crew of ten."

Your point? I thought as I shook from lack of sleep and too much caffeine. *Don't tell me I can't do it. By the way, do we have anything stronger than coffee made with redbull? I'm jonesin.*

So, I appointed myself the "Queen of Overwhelm." It wasn't a title I wanted, and it wasn't a crown I wore with pride. It was a role that happened to me, and I felt bound by it.

When I managed juggling these tasks correctly, the results could be positive. We accomplished great things as a publishing team, I kept up to speed with my day job, and life, for the most part, stayed together. Until it didn't.

I cycled through resentment fueled by burnout. blamed the world and everyone in it except me. Overwhelm pulled me underwater, anchoring my feet to the seafloor. I struggled to breathe, until I'd find a burst of motivation and get all frenzied. Pretending like I was catching up (I wasn't), every word off my tongue sounded like an inspirational poster in a company break room.

"The more you expect, the more you achieve." (Bleh, I could vomit.) "It doesn't get easier, you just get better." (It does get easier.) "If you think you can, you will!" (You can't think your way to becoming a pink elephant, though.)

My role as the Queen of Overwhelm was clearly not sustainable. So, I got a business coach. I'd done this on my own for long enough. I needed direction from someone who had a successful business: someone to be the clear guide to my journey through the jungle.

One of the first things she noticed about me was how overwhelmed I always was. From the time I woke until the time I went to bed—and I'm talking on the *daily*—I was overwhelmed about something going on in my work. I wore it like a badge, carried around the feeling on my face and in my unbrushed hair. I was proud to have built a business that was overwhelming. That meant it was working, right?

I remember the first time my coach told me, "Myra, overwhelm is a choice."

I also remember rolling my eyes from my end of the phone thinking, *Okay sure, but there's no way I chose to get into this mess. I wanted a successful business, not one that's slowly killing me. This woman is crazy, I can't just decide not to be overwhelmed.*

Of course, she was right. So, I followed her advice and tried to stop choosing to be overwhelmed. For months on end, I was like, "Yeah, I'm trying to choose not to be overwhelmed, but this feeling won't fuck off."

I didn't want the nasty feeling that came with overwhelm. You know, your stomach tenses and you get an instant phantom headache about the pressures of the world? I didn't want that shit. No matter how hard I tried to choose *not* to be overwhelmed, it kept crawling back into my life. I may not have chosen it, but it sure chose me.

You know what? I never once said "No" to the overwhelming workload.

As soon as I got honest with myself, I realized an important truth. Yes. I had every ability to choose whether or not to be overwhelmed with work, but it never lasted. I always picked the work back up. Sometimes a period of rest taught me a lot. Yet the peaceful times never taught me more than when I was buried in my overwhelm. I chose the path of overwhelm, and that path was a thick mess to get through, but it was also the path to my greatest growth.

Yup, I forged through a path of *most* resistance here, but I did choose it. Full of mangled trees and thick, scratching foliage, it was my path to bushwhack my way through. I got stronger with each bushwhack (don't you *love* that word? I had to use it twice) and found the more challenging adventure was always worth the personal growth that came along with it.

Awesome. Now what?

If overwhelm was a choice, and I consistently chose to keep it in my life, then was I doomed to having a hard life? Was I forcing myself through a lifetime of bushwhacking (it's a great word, right?) that I would soon grow weary from once more? Was I *choosing* pain? And if so, there must've been something *really* wrong with me. I must've been an accomplishment masochist.

Then, our pastor gave a sermon about leaning to "persevere for your purpose."

(Our church is the shit. I probably shouldn't use the word "shit" with the word "church" in the same sentence; I seriously doubt most religious leaders would approve. But my pastor would—at least in this context he probably would, I'm basing this on pure assumption—which further proves my point. If you're ever in my area, look me up. You can sit next to me.)

He shed light on the idea that our purpose doesn't come without some pressure. The couch isn't very overwhelming, but few people have found their purpose sinking into a pile of suede either.

If you're praying to get into college, you shouldn't expect to ace every class and hold your new part time job seamlessly and without effort. If you're praying to be a parent, you shouldn't also expect it to come without the loss of sleep and abundance of baby poo. If I was praying for a hugely successful business, I couldn't also have substantial time off in the first two years and no challenges. Basic, right? Well-practiced? Rarely.

Our pastor yell-preached about how to handle the pressure and live gracefully through those challenging times, by no means encouraging everyone to become Queens of Overwhelm. From his sermon, I took away permission to give myself a full plate *and* grace.

I realized that overwhelm didn't happen *to* me. It happened *for* me. I couldn't have a successful business without all the work. So instead of being pulled down by the nasty feelings surrounding my overwhelm, I rose up and looked at my workload, spending time fishing through my priorities to create a plan.

Work might not be your source of overwhelm. Maybe you're a new mom, and you ugly cry on the couch every day because your sister-in-law comes rollin' up to your Sunday family dinners with her well-dressed kids who behave all night with little need for discipline. Your child, on the other hand, ate a crayon before you could get it off the floor and caused mayhem in the pots and pans cupboard during the dessert course. Your SIL makes it look so easy. There must be something right with her and wrong with you!

Wanna know how she makes it look so easy? She's been where you are. She ugly cried on her couch too. Her kids ate the dust bunnies from under the furniture. She lost sleep while covered in refused-yet-partially-chewed broccoli. She even went through seven different discipline methods until she figured out what worked for each of her kids. Your sister-in-law clawed her way through parenting like the rest of us.

She makes it look easy because she fought like hell to get through the hard stuff, like you're doing now. Just because she has it "all together" now doesn't mean it was any easier on her when she was where you are. Is she called to her purpose as a parent any more than you are? No way, but isn't it interesting that it's a hell of a lot easier see someone else's purpose than it is to see our own?

Now, I don't know *your* sister-in-law personally, but we all know that person who makes something look so easy. Life is like literature, and a book that's easy to read is very damn hard to write. Don't compare someone else's chapter 10 to your chapter 2 and think you're doing something wrong for not being as far ahead. You just need to keep practicing your craft.

Are you overwhelmed? Good. It probably means you're stretching your life into something bigger.

Overwhelmed by your kids? I am, but I also want each one of those little buggers and dream fondly of the day they'll leave the house without me having to tell them twenty times to put on socks and shoes. I plan on raising the most amazing kids I can who will be kind, creative, innovative thinkers and who will change their world.

Overwhelmed by work? I am, but I also have big goals. My goals are bigger than your average bear's and I'm not going to achieve them by hibernating in my cave and complaining that there's too much foam and not enough vanilla on my honey. Don't be the kind of person who asks God for a thriving business and then complains about all the work involved.

Overwhelmed by the responsibilities in your life? You could live a life of no responsibilities, but from my experience, that isn't much of a life.

But… (Remember our brontosaurus-sized but?) But, there's another choice that accompanies overwhelm.

Yes, you can decide to keep your overwhelm and make it a valid choice. You aren't limited to just picking whether or not to be overwhelmed. You also get to determine what you want to be overwhelmed *by*.

Do I want to be overwhelmed with my kids? Or do I want to be overwhelmed with my love for them and passion for raising them right?

Do I want to be overwhelmed with my work? Or do I want to be overwhelmed by my brazen tenacity to walk directly into the storm, knowing that my dream awaits me on the other side?

We get that which we focus on, right? So, to get to my dreams, I needed to lean into the overwhelm, choosing to look at it through a better lens and focus on being overwhelmed by the good.

And that's a choice I can get behind.

So, yeah. This book is about letting go of our curse words. You know what? Fuck it. I'm going to keep this one.

I am going to keep my overwhelm, I'm just going to make sure it doesn't keep me.

Start Small(ish)

Sweet.

Are you twiddling your thumbs now? I mean, I just told you *I* wasn't going to ditch this curse word, so what could possibly be coming next?

Because I'm leaving this "curse word" in my life, giving a few tips on it is more important than ever. If you're going to choose overwhelm (otherwise known as the pressure that comes with your purpose), how do you do it without going bonkers?

For starters, don't create more pressure than is necessary. You can't spread your energy out too far; you need to narrow it to be effective. If you have a high school reunion next week, are you really going to be able to find your dream job, whittle your waist, and cyber-stalk the entire graduating class of 1998? Okay, this cliché example is extreme, but we often treat our lives like this and wonder why every growth moment comes at a snail's pace. We're spread too damn thin to make effective changes in all areas.

Take the holidays, for instance. If you're a mom, you know the sometimes unspoken rule that we are supposed to take the bulk of the planning, decorating, shopping, cooking, organizing, and wear stupid-big grins the whole time while sipping on our mint mocha with carefully painted lips because pictures are in an hour and we need to be both alert and perfect, even if we're really damn tired. Ah, it's crazy out there during the holidays. Can I get an amen?

Sure, another extreme, but what about the week in the middle of August when you have to be the perfect PTA attendee while assembling outfits for your kids for picture day while juggling a healthy home-cooked menu for the week and getting that project done before your co-worker so he doesn't get the promotion over you. Then, you have to feel like shit because you've been blowing off your friends and your kid says he wishes you were more like Matt's mom and you have to lock yourself in the bathroom to sneak a cookie and cry.

Why do we do it to ourselves?

We don't have to be it all. We can allow ourselves grace.

My advice? Edit your life relentlessly. Look at what you're trying to achieve and take an accurate look at how long each achievement will take. Then add tax. (In other words, leave room for grace.) If something is too overwhelming and it doesn't serve you and your big purpose, then decide if it really needs to be there. It's okay to be overwhelmed by an area or two of your life, then consider if it would benefit you to give yourself grace in other areas.

We can't afford to do it all with our time, so guard your time wisely and bat away the rest of the crap like an Italian football goalie.

We can't blast forward on all cylinders all the time. But…

Be Careful How You Design Your Life

There's also a danger that runs with this "extreme" of piling on as much of life as possible. Many people who shy away from overwhelm do it because they're afraid they'll take it too far and become Myra circa 2017. Yeah, I don't recommend many people becoming me from last year, but it honestly isn't the worst thing in the world. It helped me grow, brought me to a spiritual tipping point, and the wisdom I take from my year of hell will serve me for the rest of my life.

For someone to say they don't think overwhelm is healthy *at all* is saying we are incapable of learning extreme lessons from extreme situations. Perhaps their belief is limited, or they're projecting their fears onto us. Look, even if you do get as overwhelmed as I did—and you probably won't—it hasn't all been bad. I've grown, I've reprioritized, I'm no longer burning the candle at both ends, and I fucking love life.

There are tools to help make things easier. You can get better at whatever you're overwhelmed about. Let's put it this way: did you know how to ride a bike before you knew how to ride a bike? Of course not. You needed to experience it first, do some trial-and-error, get support, use training wheels, believe in yourself, and pedal like your frightened little life depended on it. After you fall, you'll get back up.

If you put in the effort, you can be great.

You also get to choose how much effort to put in.

More importantly, you get to choose where to go, and why you're going there. Find your sweet spot—the balance between "too scared to pile on the extra" and Myra circa 2017—and you'll be fine.

Consider Your Intentions

Someone once said to me (in the most loving way possible, I'm sure), "If the devil can't make you bad, he'll make you busy!"

Have you ever heard that? Where did that nonsense come from? I mean, what a weird thing to say to someone. Above not being true, it's also totally strange, right?

The statement implies that only underwhelmed people are Godly, or that being busy is as sinful as being "bad." It implies that busyness only comes from a place of evil. It implies that I want to punch you in the throat for suggesting such nonsense in the first place.

If we were made in God's image, and God made this world, then please, by all means, tell me God wasn't busy building the universe in six days and busy resting on the seventh. I'm sorry, I refuse to believe we were created to do any less than find our own purpose and pursue it with everything we've got. And yes, that makes me busy. And no, I'm not an evil bastard for choosing it.

When God intended to make the earth, God got to work.

When the enemy intended to destroy the earth, the enemy got to work.

Both got busy. Each had a different intention.

If you can have an honest conversation with yourself about your intentions and how your desired outcome will affect you and those around you, then you can make a proper judgment on what to do and how much of it to pile on your plate.

Don't Panic Under Pressure

If the value is rising and there's a present danger of blowing up under pressure, that's a good indication to step back and take a look at your life objectively. I mean, right in the middle of chaos seems like the *worst* time to step away for a bird's eye view, but you cannot make proactive decisions when you're running from one reactive fire to another.

Okay, let's example this up so you don't think I'm a nutter. Let's say you're bathing your kids. I don't know your kids, yet there's a really good chance they're like mine in the water-pouring-on-the-head department. I don't know a child alive under the age of four who holds still when you try to rinse their shampoo-soaked hair.

It doesn't matter how many times you shush them gently and promise not to get it in their eyes. It doesn't matter if you use your hand as a visor to keep the bathwater from stinging their eyes and gargling up their noses. They're going to wiggle, resist, and maybe even cry about it. Right?

Washing soap out of a child's hair isn't a big deal to the mom. It's life or death to a three-year-old.

Going through a financial crunch isn't a big deal in the grand scheme of life. Yet it seems like life or death when we have to decide between groceries or paying bills on time, right?

The breakup you experienced feels like a wretched pile of shit. When you meet the right person a year from now, it isn't going to feel like life or death anymore.

Whatever you're dealing with now, unless it's one of those key moments in life that never leave us like losing a loved one or fighting an illness, you will get through it, and it won't seem like a big deal next year.

"*OMG*, Myra. You're so insensitive!" you protest. "This shit is *hard*."

Trust that I'm wearing my most apologetic face right now while I shrug my shoulders. No one promised that life would be easy. As soon as I realized it was okay for shit not to be easy, I figured out how to lean my head back into the water gracefully. Again, I'm not discounting those super fucking hard things like losing your loving mom to cancer or having your spouse leave you for someone else. There are so many terrible things in life, and they're hell to go through.

When *not* dealing with the absolute shit parts of life, we often let pressures crush us that shouldn't even get our full emotional attention.

Please, for the love of cookie dough ice cream and everything that is right in the world, listen to this: You are greater than the problem you think is crushing you. You can get through it with some clumsy grace, and then next time, you'll get through a similar situation with *total* grace. Then, one day, someone will be ugly crying about you because you "made it look so easy." And when that happens, you have full permission to pat them on the back, give them a copy of this book and tell them to lean their heads back into the warm water.

Rest

If you need to, rest. When you're tired or weary, when your pillow is soaked with tears, rest. It's good to take moments—days, weeks sometimes—to get ourselves right, especially in between that really heavy shit life throws at us.

So, if you need to, rest.

Just don't quit.

That's all.

"ALWAYS" & "NEVER"
Every Fucking Time

I once tattooed a portrait of the Backstreet Boys on someone…
on purpose.

Bet you didn't think I was going to go *there*, didja?

In my early twenties, I started a career as a tattoo artist. I hesitate to
bring it up, because it just isn't my passion anymore, although I remain
fond of the time I spent spreading my artistic love to others and giving
them beautiful pieces. I no longer believe it was ever meant to be my
lifelong gig, and I'm okay with that. I sure as hell had fun with it, though.

Since I wasn't a big scary dude with cigarette breath, I usually worked in the front of the shop when I wasn't slinging ink or sterilizing tubes in the autoclave. I got to interact with people from all walks, answer tons of questions, and help be the face for a trending rise of female artists. The questions were never-ending, and I had an answer ready for most of them.

The only time I was at a true loss for words was when a man asked about commissioning a coverup for two names on his back. I did coverups all the time, so no biggie. Names are common cover ups, and a pro artist can make it disappear in the pedals of a flower or shading of a skull.

According to him, "This one is the name of my current girlfriend's sister, and this one is my current girlfriends' cousin." After we discussed options, he asked me (with the kind of naive sincerity I still can't stop giggling about) how much it would cost to add his current girlfriend's name to the fresh tattoo.

I'll admit, I was stumped. Not that I couldn't price out my work, but because I wasn't going to be involved, knowingly, in the drama he was probably causing this poor family. Thankfully, another artist spoke up and recommended getting the family's last name tattooed, so he could just make is way around the rest of the aunts, cousins, and maybe even the mom. (One of the best laughs I've ever had in my life. Needless to say, we didn't work on him.)

Other than the random weird ones, the most common question I got was, "Do you ever get nervous before a tattoo?"

Totally valid question. If you're going to put permanent ink on your skin, you better get it done by a pro who doesn't convulse with fear.

My response, like clockwork, was, "Never."

And, for the most part, it was true. I always felt comfortable behind a tattoo machine. Even when I was a fledgling, practicing on volunteers (and myself), I would describe my serious pre-tattoo demeanor as "Michael Phelps before a Rio race." I wouldn't ever call it "nervous."

I was content with the use of the word "never." Then one day, I was approached about doing a portrait tattoo. I'd done portraits before, usually sweet little baby faces with a banner and a birth date. I wasn't what you would call a "realistic portrait artist," though I could make baby cheeks pop. This, however, was not a request for a black and grey rendition of Junior on a forearm. My sweet new friend asked me to permanently tattoo half her back with four grown-ass, recognizable men in full color.

I've never been nervous to take on a challenge, and apparently, I thought I was invincible, so I took the job. She was the absolute sweetest person alive and didn't have a problem talking me into it. As a successful single woman in her fifties, my client had been a Backstreet Boys fan since their debut. She attended multiple concerts, served as the president of a fan club chapter for a while, and basically didn't give a fuck what anyone thought. I applauded her tenacity and welcomed the chance to learn more while I carefully tattooed these pop icons for *hours* on her back.

I was happy with the outcome—they were recognizable *as* the four remaining members, so that was good. Not to mention my first color tattoo of multiple people worked without one looking like a self-tanning addict or something. And she loved it. I mean, I've never seen anyone more over the moon about a tattoo in my whole career, and I've seen some tattoos give serious emotional healing.

Her enthusiasm was contagious, and I rejoiced in a job well done. It had been a weird request—and remains the strangest tattoo I've ever done unless you count the time I was begged to tattoo a wispy shadow on a man's stomach that he intended to look like a six-pack. Weird can be wonderful, right? To each their own. I was content nodding finely at my work and moving onto the next masterpiece.

Untillll… the photo surfaced online. And why wouldn't it?

As a prominent member of the BSB community, she proudly displayed her shoulder for anyone to photograph. And though most people seemed miffed more by the content than the artwork, there were some who shredded both. "Why would a tattoo artist *do* that to someone?" was a common phrase in the comment threads. I went down a rabbit hole of online searches, reading these one-line zingers written by miserable, judgmental people who probably had cartoon characters scratched into *their* ankle. (Sorry, the bitterness creeps back sometimes.)

I let the opinions of others seep into my identity so much that I began to believe I had "never" been a good tattoo artist. I started saying things like, "I always fuck it up" and "I'll never be good at that style."

I let my confidence drag, and therefore wasn't producing my best work. I even started charging people less money. I'd overpromise and underdeliver (sound familiar as a Myra-pattern?), and I soon realized I didn't enjoy the work anymore. I stopped tattooing for a long time. Well, only a few months, but in tattoo time, that's at least five years.

During this time, I illustrated a kid's book for a dear friend who was self-publishing her little pumpkin masterpiece. It was so much fun to be artistic again, especially when I could start over with a clean sheet of paper if I messed up. I was a new mom, and so I juggled my time between applesauce and colored pencils, but I completed the project, and my new client was happy.

I rediscovered the joy of creating art, and that felt pretty good. I had also revealed something even greater—my new love for creating books.

I went back to tattooing for a while, and I even got my verve back. But the break that resulted from a mortifying experience actually bred a new dream.

The bottom line was I did the best job I could when asked to do the tattoo, just as I did with the children's book illustrations, and both clients loved the result. In fact, my tattoo client loved her Backstreet Boys tattoo so much that when the fifth member rejoined the group for a tour a few years later, she flew 1,004.1 miles to have me add the other guy's face, along with all their signatures. Hear that? I had done my job so successfully that she came back for more. Even though I spent several years in between believing the lie that I wasn't good anymore.

She even went on a cruise with the BSBs and got their approval and a picture with them to prove it. (And yes, you can find it by Googling it. Last I checked, it was still on the first page of results, so have at it.)

Words like "always" and "never" can be poisonous. By placing one before a statement that is true for a *single* situation convinces our brain that it is true for all situations. We can rewrite our histories to reflect our beliefs. I did one tattoo in my whole career that got slammed publicly, yet I rewrote my history by convincing myself *all* my pieces were terrible and not worth the money I charged.

Even though I've carefully combed my words to be non-offensive (most of the time) and considered them for maximum effect, I know someone can fire off a blasting review at any time. When that happens (I'm not wishing it, I'm just aware that even Disneyland has bad reviews) I can either convince myself that my writing sucks for all eternity, or I can choose to see it as a singular event.

And yeah, I tend to say the wrong thing sometimes, but that doesn't mean I always do.

Just because you fucked up once doesn't mean you should identify yourself as a "fuck up" forever.

Replace Your Curse Words

You've probably heard the saying "You can't eradicate your old habits, you can only replace them with new ones," or something to that effect. I'm not sure if that's true for all occasions; let's run with it for this one.

There are two very powerful words you can swap out instead of using, "always" and "never." You can literally pluck out the demon words above and drop in these new ones and your whole life will change. I'll tell you what they are in a minute.

First, I must be super obnoxious and gush about my love for comedy. I'm not personally all that funny—or, at least, I have the kind of humor that *I* think is hilarious—but I cannot get enough of the stuff. If I was stuck on a desert island and could only pick three survival tools, I'd choose a hatchet, some TP, and Netflix so I'd never be short of stand-up comedy. I mean, I'd probably toss the misogynistic comedians to the sharks (they still, shockingly, exist) but I'd keep the ones who are generally respectful. Don't even get me started with my love of *SNL* and other sketch comedy shows and punk shows on TV (as long as they're appropriate), and improv. Oh, how I love improv when it's good.

Once, when my husband and I were exhausted after a day of spring snowboarding and I was delirious from all the sun and Bloody Marys, I had this epiphany as to why I loved comedy. I was berserk, and so I dictated the thought into my phone. I'll clean it up for you (mostly because the dictate feature on my phone refuses to recognize cussing). The edited gist is this:

"Comedy is the most poetic love letter of life. It is the devotion to and the elevation from the injustices we refuse to see in the world. The ultimate restraint of anger isn't silence—it's humor. Humor takes the pain felt by inequality, and instead of silencing it or screaming the kind of protest that is so loud no one listens, comedy dwells on the injustice and morphs it from a dark place, making the solutions reachable."

My love for laughter runs deep, even if the funniest thing I'll ever say is that one joke I shouldn't tell in public. Other than the obvious deeper lessons of comedy, there's a simple lesson to be found. There's a standard rule in improv comedy theater. When a group of comedians are on stage, improvising a scene, anything can happen. You think you're acting out a skit about a guy who's lost his girlfriend's dog, and suddenly, the mailman enters and says, "I didn't find your dog, but here's the alligator you said went missing from the zoo."

What? What the hell just happened? You definitely said you were looking for a dog.

Sounds kind of like life, right?

You, as the comedian, have two choices in this situation, and only one of them is viable. If you say, "No, I never said that," you've killed the scene. The audience won't connect with the story and you've killed the validity to the humor your opponent was attempting.

The *only* way to react to any improv situation is by saying, "Yes, and…"

"Why YES, I reported that alligator missing last week, AND it must've ate the dog!"

"I'm never a good parent" becomes, "Yes, I made a mistake a few days ago when I let myself get so stressed that I took it out on my kids and yelled at them so loud I was afraid my neighbor would wonder about me. *And*, I'm a good mom who then apologized to my kids, showing them that even mommies make bad choices sometimes."

"I always get passed over for promotions" becomes, "Yes, I've been undervalued in the past. And I choose to learn from each situation and find my own way, a better way."

No matter what your "always" and "never" is, you can recognize the pain point and allow yourself enough grace to be constructive. There is beauty in the subtlety of life that we only see it if we stop to look at each situation as its own opportunity. Don't lump everything bad together and smash your bad experiences into your hair like mud and then wonder why your head hurts.

Let bad days be bad days; don't let them turn into a bad life.

The Good "Always" and "Never"

You've probably punched a hole in my argument by now to the tune of "those words aren't all bad," and you're right. We can use them to manage our futures.

I will never cheat on my husband. Never. I will always love my kids. Always.

The difference is that words like "always" and "never" are only poisonous if the ones that follow speak death and not life. When given the option, always speak life into people, situations, and (definitely) into yourself.

"What's she talking about with this 'speak life' bullcrap?"

It's easy:

"I'm such a loser" = death talk

"I always try my best" = life talk

"I'd like to do something with my life someday, but I just don't think I'm capable" = death talk

"I may not be super smart, crazy-talented, or modelesque like so-and-so, but I'm going to try anyway" = life talk

Choose words that will lift you and others up. Speak life again, sister, and let the words that tumble from your mouth be uplifting and beautiful. Cry out for justice *and* laugh. And, instead of using extreme words to rewrite your past, use them to rewrite your future.

You have the power to do that.

NOW WHAT? Tackle Your Shit

I grew up in the golden age of sleepovers. My friends and I would gather in hoards, piling onto couches for movie marathons, popcorn, and gossip about who we thought the popular boys liked (it was always Stephanie) and how we should start styling our hair based on the newest issue of *Seventeen* magazine. Slumber parties helped me socially acclimate when I was a young and awkward, but they always came with a risk.

As a parent who's afraid that everything and anything can hurt my precious babies, I understand the parenting side of it now. When my kids are in someone else's house for the night, they must follow new rules while being respectful. This can make them question the world if, say, someone's rules are the opposite of ours. It's a lot to navigate. Peer pressure can change them, too. My sweet babies could even fall victim to the bad choices of others, simple or sinister—I don't have control, but I can't guard them forever. Eventually, I will need to let my kids grow and stand up for themselves and their beliefs. My parents also knew this, and we discussed it heavily before I was ever released to an overnight party.

With my bags packed and my imagination nearing its capacity thinking of all the fun I'd have at 2 am with my friends, my mom would sit me down for a talk about not giving in when others make bad choices. Sure, she was probably talking about not playing along if my friends decided to stick Sarah's hand in warm water because it's really damn mean to make someone pee themselves. But, I'm sure she also had bigger fears.

So, she would tell me the same thing every time. "Myra, remember who you are."

I never questioned what she meant. In those five words I heard over and over in my childhood, I understood much more. She may as well have said, "Myra, remember you are a compassionate, loving person who doesn't hurt others on purpose. You make good choices. Remember to look out for your friends and yourself, and don't forget for a moment that you have support and can call. Remember who you are, all the bits, and stay true to that person because there is only one of you."

I held firm to her words in my youth, but when I blossomed into an adult, I lost my way.

In a desperate accumulation of what I thought I wanted in life, I vanished from my true self and what was at my core. As much as this next chapter of my life is about using my curse words *for* me, and overcoming their captivity so I can fall into the path of limitlessness, I'm also determined to remember who I am.

I still hear her words in a whispering memory, "Myra, remember who you are."

You know who I am? I'm a lover of the arts. (There. I said it. Phew, what a load off.) Literature, music, theatre, visual arts, dance, tattoos, sculpting, and yes, even doodles and stick figures: It's all magic to me.

Whether from the stage of a theatre, the back corner of a pub, or through my scratchy car radio, I soak up music like an endless sponge. I don't think there's a problem in the human heart that can't be cured with the right song, or combination thereof. Remember those high school times when you'd make each other mixtapes/CDs/playlists? Close your eyes for a second and recall how it made you feel to share with someone the songs that swept you away and taught you how to feel. If you're my age or older, you can probably still picture all that time you spend hovering over your radio, waiting for the DJ to play the song you requested so you could hit "record," and how much of the joy transferred into the gift of the tape itself.

I grew up playing music and singing, yet I'd let it go since leaving college. My mom's gentle reminder faded, and I allowed a piece of me to disappear. One failed audition too many, I convinced myself I couldn't love singing if someone else told me I wasn't good enough to do it in front of a crowd.

Until a few years ago, when my wonderful dad gifted me a ukulele for Christmas, and my love affair with playing and singing was rekindled. It was like being able to read a language I forgot I was fluent in. I learned, like, thirty songs in a week after picking it up, and I found infinite comfort in the simple pluck of the nylon strings. Captivated by my ability to strum out my childhood favorites, I lost myself in a sea of James Taylor, Stevie Nicks, and Ella Fitzgerald all over again. The songs came out of my mouth and off my fingers, and the creation of these mini-music-vacations I created for my family at dinnertime kept me alive inside through the hard times.

I love music, so I'm committed to play and sing more of it... maybe in front of an audience someday soon (gulp). I may never qualify for anything more than an occasional open mic, but I'm done pretending that I don't have a voice that I love to use.

And God, I love a good book. Like, *love* a good story. So, I'm going to write more of them and read more of them. I get to sink into a story like I'm living a different life every day. It's enchanting and adventurous and conducive to growth, all wrapped up in an eloquent bow of delicately chosen words. Good thing I chose this industry to get into, right?

And poetry? That shit is DE-*licious*.

And, although I still love a beautiful tattoo and spending time painting or drawing, I've fallen out of love with the production of it. Not all the way; visual art will always be a part of my life, and someday it may become more important to me again. For now, I'm content enjoying it the way I enjoy a good movie or theatre production; I'll support by contributing to the audience size.

Why should you care about my love of the arts?

I'm not trying to get you to donate to your local arts program of choice (though it'd be cool if you did). I'm saying this because years ago, my artistic landscape was different. And in another decade, my loves will have changed again. And that's okay. There is nothing wrong with me for changing my path and becoming a "newbie" in something I've always wanted to try. Not everyone can and will pursue one single vision for their life.

Maybe we're discontent with life because we're not chasing a time-appropriate dream. When I was tattooing, I spent all my extra time sketching, illustrating, and immersing myself in the art world to keep up with trends and deepen my study of color theory. I wouldn't have imagined that my career in that field would be short-lived, replaced by one significantly more fulfilling.

I've allowed these different arts to come and go, flowing into my life and out giving me exactly what I need from the beautiful experience. In ten years, I could be a set designer or a sculptor. But I'll never not have the arts in my life; they're too damn amazing.

I've also dreamed up ideas that never happened. I've seen others in my life do the same, and I know the vision and fire we can all have for a dream we're sure will come true, only to watch our idea fizzle with the passing of time and lack of opportunity. So often, we take those disappointments from an unfulfilled vision and view it as failure. And what I know to be true about failure is that most people don't just identify themselves as someone who has *had* a failure, they assume the identity and *become* a failure.

Wake up, 7-up.

You have this great big beautiful world surrounding you, and it's full of opportunities and new dreams. They're not all going to pan out the way you anticipate but *come on*. Since when has sheltering yourself from your potential become the cool thing?

(I'm going to take a deep breath here and say this quickly. It'll be like ripping off a Band-Aid.)

We've settled.

Yup. It's worth repeating, *we've settled.*

Somewhere along the way, we shrugged ourselves into a life that was less than what we wanted because we started believing we were these goddamn curse words. You don't have to be your curse words anymore. You can let them go.

I'll even promise you something: If you're the type of person who freaks at the thought of not being bound to a negative identity—because who would you *be?* You're known as the "irritable one" in your circle of friends. If you changed that, you may not have an identity left!

If that's you, you'll find other curse words to struggle with in the future, so don't worry. Maybe you currently struggle with feeling fragile, and once you navigate your way through it, you find a butt-ton of anxiety on the other side. Lean into it and keep growing. If—nay, *when*—that happens, know that nothing is wrong with you and that life isn't an endless battle of negative treachery.

Please don't subconsciously excuse yourself from growing because, "Well, once I solve one problem, another is right around the corner." Of course, there's more trouble waiting for you. This is life, not heaven. There are more than seven billion of us to bump around and emotionally affect. Pair that with Murphy's Law and our own general lack of perfection (otherwise known as "the human condition"), and we're always going to have some trials to face. Troubles aren't going to go away.

Doesn't it seem like the more we face trials and tribulations, the better we get at navigating future ones? Instead of focusing on making a problem go away, set your sights on what you can learn from the problem. If you've got to go through it, get something out of it.

Then, you will walk into your next trial with more emotional maturity. Life is going to give us challenges—that's a given. Treating these issues as inconveniences will keep you stuck, whereas growing through each challenge will raise you up. You can continue to dance through life implementing changes and then acclimating to them without the chronic fear of defaulting into negativity.

And, if you're one of those people—like me and everyone else, even if they won't raise their hand—who has gone through challenges and fell on your epic little face, then fear not! Even if you've sucked at some shit and didn't learn anything from it, (and probably curse the whole idea of that situation, no matter how many people push you to "face it and find closure") you still have a future ahead of you. In other words, no matter how much you fucked up, you can overcome and thrive.

I don't know, maybe you did meth for a long time, and it rotted your mouth so bad that you can barely stand to smile, even though you're trying to be the best recovering addict and new mom you can be. Maybe you're still judged, even though that's not who you are anymore. You've worked your ass off to get in a stable place, yet you can't even comprehend building yourself up any higher when people dismiss you before they even talk to you.

No matter what the past has held for you, you are the only one who can say "yes" to being released from bondage. Is the road ahead going to be easy? Hell no. Ugh, it breaks my heart to even say that, but just because something isn't going to be easy doesn't mean it isn't epic, beautiful, fulfilling, and rewarding.

Maybe every time you overhear a mom in the pickup line whisper "meth mouth" under her breath, instead of letting it hurt you, you let it fuel you to help change the image of what a recovering addict looks like. Perhaps you even get involved at a local nonprofit, even if you're the glorified envelope stuffer. Instead of letting your (very valid) fears silence you, you get your words out however you can and find that you love writing moving proposals. After years of observing how addicts and recovering addicts are treated, you know exactly what to say to expose the truth of their pain and injustice. So, *maybe* you take an online course on how to write grant proposals.

Just because it's hard to understand at first doesn't mean you can't acquire new skills. Test yourself out and see how far you can go with dreams, taking just the step in front of you and then the next. Don't forget: no one said you have to do it alone. I bet you could find support at your local church; I've met some of the most amazing cheerleaders at church.

You spend several weeks crafting your first copy of your grant proposal and show it to the lady you volunteer under. She's kind of a twat about the whole thing because she thinks you're after her job, but you don't let it stop you.

Just because you hit a roadblock right out of the gates doesn't mean it's the wrong path for you to walk down. Don't take every hardship as an excuse to stop. Just because it's hard doesn't mean it isn't your destiny.

You pivot, and now you have a new mission. You schedule a time to meet with the owners of the non-profit and show them your writing sample. They see potential and boom! It's a start. Keep moving until you reach the next obstacle, and then press in and pivot, finding another way. Before you know it, you'll have all the options you need to reach your goal, and the beauty of the journey will likely encapsulate you in the confidence, joy, and fulfillment you've been seeking.

And maybe, after years obstacle-jumping and ignoring the word "No," you find yourself running that non-profit company, serving others and making a healthy living that has afforded you the ability to own a home, send your babies to college, and yes, replace your damaged teeth.

You can formulate your own scenario here. Maybe you can imagine someone staring down the sharp, jagged edges of a mental illness or trauma. Or you know that divorced gal whose spouse left her in emotional shambles and piles of debt. Or you can turn your hypothetical solution-making to a family member who you can *surely* help if she'd only listen to your advice.

I love the study of people: what makes them tick, what their intentions are, why they do what they do. If you look carefully, you can see hints of this in every piece of art that exists. And I'll be the first to admit that I like to "solve" other people's problems for them in my head. I used to think it was a bad habit, but it's normal. I think we like to theorize what's best for others for two reasons. 1) Our brains are practicing for when we have to do our own problem solving, and 2) There's no personal responsibility when composing a hypothetical solution. Oh, and who could forget 3) Because we're compassionate people who want what's best for others. Having an opinion about what might be best for someone doesn't make us monsters, but without the empathy and depth of understanding about their situation, we can't always trust that our opinion will be considered or is even welcomed.

Nevertheless, we can *see* the end of other people's finish lines much easier than our own. We see their purpose because we're not lost in their problems. We see solutions for them because there's no investment for us to simply imagine it.

Could I be so bold as to suggest that you could look objectively at your own life? See where you're hindering yourself, being stifled, losing energy, at a dead end, not getting fulfilled, etc. If that situation were happening to a loved one, what would you recommend? Better yet, if you're a parent, imagine your kid in that situation. Would you let them work through it the way you're currently tackling the issue?

Most importantly, we must care about getting over our curse words. Put your oxygen mask on first, people. Stop your bleeding before you go rushing to save others. At least, give enough shits about yourself to prioritize your needs on occasion. It isn't too much to ask, it's necessary. You are worth the time it takes to figure some shit out.

I have this dream that you've changed a little during our time together. Maybe you just picked up a few nuggets of inspiration to carry into your life. Or perhaps you've been able to address a deeper problem, and now you're trying to navigate through adjusting the fundamentals of your life.

Whatever stage you're in—valley or climb, increase or decrease, growth or contentment—I pray that you will only use curse words to your benefit and stop identifying as them. Wring every ounce of wisdom out of your challenges and then express it by living a beautiful life. Bless others when you can, even if it's just with words. Recognize the changes you make so you can look back with gratitude for the life you've lived.

The way we deal with anything and everything boils down to choices. I hope you choose life. Every time. I hope you can love yourself enough to know what you need next, and then pursue it with everything you can. When people shovel shit on you, I wish you would shake it off and step up. Each time a dream doesn't work out, I pray that God will give you a new one; and may it be bigger and better than the last.

Most of all, I pray that you never give up. Letting go of our old self can be hard. But identifying as a "fuck up" or "piece of shit" isn't a viable alternative. Whether you come in first or last, finish your race. Whether you've been disappointed around every corner or not, find love. Even if you've been broken into a million fragile pieces, you can find grace and strength within you and those around you and can rebuild stronger.

Life is a choice.

You choose which words define you. Instead of reaching for the old standbys, "loser," "outcast," "stupid," "never enough," or whatever horrible name you've given yourself (that you would *never* give a loved one, by the way), you can choose a different word by which to be defined. You can be "blessed beyond measure," "always maturing into the wonderful creation God made you to be," or (and this one is my FAVORITE), you can be defined by your *name*.

I'm no longer a "fuck up." I'm Myra, and I remember who I am. I'm a complex mess of emotions who loves to grow and explore different things. I refuse to live with regret, and so I pursue my talents and passions relentlessly, even if others think it's foolish. Even if sometimes I think it's foolish.

I'm the only one in the world who will fulfill a Myra-Fiacco-sized purpose.

And you are the only one who can fulfill a you-sized purpose.

If you don't do it, who will?

Sister, remember who you are.

FINISHED Fucking Start

In his final words, Jesus said, "It is finished."

Terminado.

Fertig.

Finito.

Fini.

Finished.

We all know what happened next. If you've been around the story of Jesus for five minutes, you know that he bled and died. You also know he was buried in a borrowed tomb, where his dead body lay for three days. And what happened next?

You can all say it with me—He rose again.

I had heard the story of Jesus more times than I ever thought was necessary, until that time I experienced my self-death in the basement while talking to God. About to lose my grip on reality completely, I cried out to God to save me from myself. After it happened, I felt like a toddler learning to walk, like a tourist in an unknown land. Everything felt new and weird, but I liked it.

I went back to church. Every song spoke to my heart and drew forth a well of happy tears I thought was dry. Every word had new meaning, and I gobbled up each phrase until I was spiritually fat and ready to get through the upcoming weeks.

Eventually, with my old-self amputated, I began to stop "getting through" the week, and I started "triumphing through" the week. I got my thrive on and I'm now on a mission to help others find theirs.

I stood beside that shriveled version of "old me" in the train station of my mind that night and said, "It is finished." It was finished, but I wasn't done. I found a new life with God and observed the death of my darkness, but I've still got work to do.

When you feel like you're "finished," girl, that's just the beginning. Being finished is beautiful; it's an amputation of the old, it's a dormant rose bush that will come back, it's a move to a new city, it's a new career path or a new relationship. We should all look for our moments of being "finished," because what follows is life, *real* life that is happening right now.

Next time you say, "I'm done—I can't do this anymore because it's killing me," look at what is on the other side of being finished. There's life over there, tons of it, and it's beautiful and waiting for you. You may think you're "finished," but you've only just begun. Beautiful, right?

So, I only have one more thing to say: Thank you.

Thank you, dear sister, for being a part of my journey. Not everyone who has gone through a breakthrough has documented it and having had the ability to do so takes my spiritual breath away. I'm honored to share the darkness in me if it means you got to see the light, too.

If you're on the "Myra circa 2017" side of things, I beg you to keep pieces of it; whether you're into writing, journaling, creating art, or explaining your thoughts and emotions through music or dance. Better yet, chronicle the whole thing, even before you get there. Pre, during, and post-breakthrough, if you are determined to share your experience and pass it along, I believe we can change the world we live in. I can't do it alone, but we can start a movement.

Did you know there's a word for the dumping of the darkness? There's a single word that fully encompasses the breakthroughs of this world— the pain before the progress, the beauty of the during, and the explosive creation on the other side of glory and literally everything in between. Just one word that strings together all emotions into a connective, expressive thread:

Art.

We are all artists of our own craft. Whether your art is done on the stage or in a lab, at your child's bedside as you read them their favorite book (and do the voices even though you're tired because you're a badass) or in front of a stove as you whip together a culinary masterpiece. Find your art. Discover it and cultivate it. My art is writing and music. Yours might be street art or body work (cars, massage, painting, whatever). Perhaps it's digital design or drawing up contracts.

Get your ideas out—your emotions, opinions, pains and trials—in your appropriate medium. Dump your feelings into your drawing, your writing, your performance. Work through your shit in a tangible way and you'll inspire others to do the same.

The most successful pieces of art are raw.

You. You're a piece of art, and your greatest beauty can come out of your rawness.

I don't want to just encourage you to be artistic in a few words and then never follow up. That'd be insane. Y'all have so much in you. So much. Each one has a beauty that is unlike what anyone else can create. Our world is better because you're a part of it. This book is proof that there's more to me than what one might see in passing on the street.

Show the world that there's more in you, too.

Share your art, share your story of being finished and starting new.

It is finished, and yet…

It's only the beginning.

Now go, create, and use your curse words. They're done using you.

&@#%$!

I challenge you to join the #UsingCurseWords movement.

Join me on social media using the hashtag #UsingCurseWords to show how you used your curse word for art. Send a picture, video, or audio clip, or description of your creations. By flooding the world with our exquisite rawness in art, we can champion those alongside us.

Help me show the world how much you matter.

Help me show the world how much the person next to you matters.

We can fight for each other, and we'll use our fucking curse words to do it.

Sister, I got your back.

Let's fucking do this...

#USINGCURSEWORDS
Join the Movement

Hop on your favorite social media platform and use the hashtag **#UsingCurseWords** to tag your art, poetry, photography, etc. Show the world what you've created and boast about how you're working through your shit and using your curse words instead of letting them use you.

Tag @MyraFiacco and don't forget the hashtag.

We'll select a post every day to feature on UsingCurseWords.com, which will then be shared to the author and publishing company's large platforms.

AuthorMyraFiacco	# UsingCurseWords
@MyraFiacco	UsingCurseWords.com
MyraFiacco	contact@myrafiacco.com

A special note about sharing your art: Remember your audience; this is a public platform. Some art is very private. So, if you wish to contribute but question the appropriateness of your art or want it to be shared anonymously, you are welcome to email me. We will share it for you, respecting your privacy.

Disclaimer: Please don't dump your agony into a rock ballad and then scream-sing it for your kid's preschool; find your audience. Again, if you aren't sure who your audience is but would like to contribute, we'll gladly be your gatekeeper. Email me and the team and we'll help you determine your audience.

AKNOWLEDGEMENTS
Shit-ton of Thanks

I wrote this fast and furiously, capturing the lessons I learned as soon as I learned them (following my breakdown). Sometimes I pulled from my past, and other times I didn't. Aligning all these stories in a way that would affect readers maximumly took massive effort. So, when I say "thanks," trust me, it isn't flippant.

Jess Moore, you jumped in without question, often at a moment's notice. Your thoughtful insights helped me portray my heart without putting my foot in my mouth, and your calm confidence has always seeped into this whirlwind of a book. Thanks for being a part of this; I love working with you.

Milly Thiringer, editing this book isn't the only work you did to make this possible. I'm grateful for all our conversations, all your passions, and most of all, for helping me through the breakdown. Few people saw the extent of the shit storm, but you had a front row seat and handled your position with grace. Thanks for lifting me through my pivot point. Above all, thanks for inviting me back to church.

Megan Dailey, um… you're a rock star. Y'all, she's *so* good. I can't even. Thanks, girl.

Gabrielle Hensyel, no one helped me through like you did. You're like my fourth sister, and I love having you in my life.

Tiffany Julie. Shit girl. For helping me see how much I'm worth this, for wading through all the bullshit with me week after week, and for showing me a better way, I am so grateful. You're the leader I strive to be, and though I may have questioned your sanity the first time you encouraged me to meditate (…in spaaaaace…), you've never steered me wrong. You held my hand through the hard work—the mindset stuff—and thanks doesn't seem like a big enough word here. "Yas queen" is slightly more appropriate. So is "holy fucking shit, you're amazing." Okay, I'm done.

To Brenda and Huston Green (my mom and dad. Give it up for my folks!), I'm at a loss for how to thank you. You've shown me the world, yet you've grounded me. You've lifted me and let me fall. You've led by example but have always started me off on your shoulders. I'm dumbfounded by your love. You're both incredible human beings, and I'm blessed by you daily. Thanks for always fighting for me.

Nick. You've walked through hell with me; your love has molded me into who I am. Together, we can conquer anything, and I can't wait to see what we do next. You're my best friend, and I love you furiously and deeply. Whenever I've perched myself on the edge of a cliff, your response has always been, "We can do it together—let's fly." And fly we will.

And finally, to the reader. If you've plowed through this journey with me thus far (not many die-hard readers even stick it out through the acknowledgments), then you've seen first-hand the ripple effect we have on each other's lives. I pray you'll recognize that every encounter you have can bring life. Give thanks for all of it. Celebrate each moment. Together, we make this world wonderful.

My BIO Damn Self

Illustration credit - millythiringer.com

With a peppered history in illustration, performing arts, and professional ghostwriting, Myra brings an artistic savvy and ingenuity to the craft of publishing. She edits and publishes award-winning books for deserving authors and writes her own while growing a platform to empower her team. Striving to be a stake of support in this crazy business of publishing, Myra runs publishing support groups, workshops, and a YouTube channel. She speaks on the topic of writing and living your BEST life and loves every minute of actively driving others to fulfill their potential. Myra lives in the beautiful heart of Coeur d'Alene, ID, with her amazing family.

Above all, Myra is joyful again. And limitless. And she knows it.

REFERENCES
Know Your Shit

1. Martin, Sean. "Yellowstone volcano WARNING: Supervolcano WILL erupt and could END human civilisation" *express.co.uk.* 2018. URL: www.express.co.uk/news/world/1020850/Yellowstone-volcano-latest-news-Supervolcano-warning-eruption-volcano-news
2. ibid.
3. Kiderra, Inga. "How the Brain Makes—and Breaks—a Habit," *UC San Diego News Center.* 2016. URL: ucsdnews.ucsd.edu/pressrelease/how_the_brain_makes_and_breaks_a_habit
4. ibid.
5. Bergland, Christopher. "Your Brain Can Be Trained to Self-Regulate Negative Thinking," *Psychology Today.* 2016. URL: www.psychologytoday.com/us/blog/the-athletes-way/201601/your-brain-can-be-trained-self-regulate-negative-thinking
6. ibid.
7. Dispenza, Joe. "Official News and Fan Page" *facebook.com.* 2012. URL: www.facebook.com/DrJoeDispenzaOfficialNewsFanPage/posts/the-frontal-lobe-is-the-seat-of-our-attention-focused-concentration-aware-ness-ob/458053824220017/
8. Palmer, Amy. "The Neuroscience of Visualization," guest post on *mindmovies.com.* 2018. URL: www.mindmovies.com/blogroll/the-neuro-science-of-visualization
9. ibid.

Crisis and Mental Health Resources

National Alliance for Mental Illness
https://www.nami.org/
Crisis Line: 800-950-6264 or text **NAMI** to **741741**

Suicide Prevention Lifeline
https://suicidepreventionlifeline.org/
1-800-273-8255

Trans Lifeline (staffed by transgender individuals)
https://www.translifeline.org/
877-565-8860

SAMHSA Treatment Referral Helpline
https://www.mentalhealth.gov/get-help/immediate-help
1-877-SAMHSA7 (1-877-726-4727)
(will help you find treatment options in your area)